JESUS

Q

EVERY QUESTION
JESUS ASKED

JONAH BEN-JOSEPH

What are you looking for? (John 1:38)

~ Jesus of Nazareth

Contents

Introduction

One man, one Jew produced the greatest influence on humanity – Jesus from Nazareth. His teachings matured and evolved human understanding of God and split the universe into two: between those who accept Jesus' teachings and those who reject them. Jesus' teachings are recorded in the Bible, sacred scriptures nearly 2,000 pages long. Given that length, where should one begin reading? The best place is certainly the Four Gospels – Matthew, Mark, Luke, and John.

If you are already familiar with the Gospels, this new book – *Jesus Q – Every Question Jesus Asked* – offers a profoundly clear and straightforward way to learn more about his teachings by giving the reader a closer look at his every question.

Why is this especially helpful? Because it is by asking and answering questions that we learn. If you do not know the answer to something, ask someone who knows the answer.

There is a sense in which life can be seen as a stream of questions and answers.

Some questions are simple:

> What's your name?
> What's your cell number?
> Do you know the way to San Jose?

Some questions are routine:

> How is the project going?
> What tax code is referenced here?
> When does the book club meet?

Other questions can be life changing:

> When will the hurricane land?
> Did you get the job offer?
> What did the doctor say?
> Will you marry me?

Jesus of Nazareth asked many questions.

Some were rhetorical: "Can a blind person guide a blind person?"

Some showed his frustration: "If you do not believe me when I talk to you about earthly things, how are you to believe if I should talk about the things of heaven?"

Some of Jesus' questions were sharp: "Where is your faith?"

Whether one is a Christian, Buddhist, agnostic, or another category of believer – or even a non-believer – one will gain new insights into Jesus' teachings through hearing his questions. In *Jesus Q*, you will investigate every recorded question Jesus asked his family, friends, followers, and his adversaries.

If you are new to reading the Bible, I believe *Jesus Q* will be particularly helpful, because it advances your understanding more quickly than people who have not focused on his questions. Even students of university-level theology courses will find focusing on Jesus' questions reveals aspects of his teachings you may have missed. If you are an agnostic, *Jesus Q* is also meant for you; it can give you insights into what inspires Christians about this man from Nazareth. And for those who practice another faith, this book is also for you, because I believe it can help you understand how Jesus of Nazareth differs from leaders of other religions.

So listen to Jesus' questions.

Author's Note: Five things before you begin reading *Jesus Q*

The goal of this book is to help you ponder and discover new meaning in each question Jesus asked. Writing a book to accomplish that at first appeared a straightforward undertaking, but it soon became a much more difficult matter for five reasons:

1. Matthew, Mark, Luke and John do not always agree on the order of events that they describe, and that made it problematic to write *Jesus Q* in chronological order.

2. Matthew, Mark, Luke, and John were inspired by the Holy Spirit. Even so, they do not always agree whether Jesus had asked a question or made a statement. So it became an issue which Gospel to use in deciding if Jesus had asked a question or not.

3. Several questions that Jesus asked are so closely related to one another that it is difficult to separate them, thus presenting the problem of deciding if they are multiple questions or a single question posed by Jesus in different ways.

4. There are many versions of the Holy Bible. Which version would be the best to use for *Jesus Q*?

5. Writing is easy, but writing with insight is more difficult, and writing with insight about a holy man, who is the Son of

God, is a supremely special effort where mistakes are to be avoided at all costs.

Here is how I approached these five problems.

1. **The Four Gospels are not in chronological order.** As it is easier understanding something chronologically, it was my goal to present Jesus' questions in order. But since I used all four Gospels, a total and comprehensive chronological synchronization was not possible. Nevertheless, I have striven to place his questions in a chronological order as far as I found it possible to do so.

2. **The Gospels do not always agree whether Jesus made a statement or asked a question.** When one Gospel shows Jesus making a statement, but another Gospel shows his words as a question, I always chose the Gospel reading that showed Jesus asking a question. Thus, I sought out all of Jesus' questions, to make this book as complete as possible.

3. **Many questions Jesus asked are closely related to one another, should they be considered one question or several?** Answering this required common sense, judgment and Biblical understanding, and I employed all three in deciding if it was a separate question needing individual attention, or if it was a question that was so closely related to another question, or several other questions, that they should be understood as one question. I hope that the reader will agree with my assessments, but if one does not, that is fine.

4. **There are many English translations of the Holy Bible. Which one should be used as the best source for *Jesus Q*?** There are many excellent English versions of the Bible and Christians will usually prefer one of them to own and study. Individual taste greatly matters in making that

decision, as well as one's "ear," that is, how a particular version *sounds to you.*

In choosing which version to use, my decision was guided by the beauty, clarity and accuracy of its English. For me, the best choice is the Revised English Bible (REB) because it is widely recognized for its accuracy and graceful English. Therefore, the majority of the quotes in *Jesus Q* are from the REB. (Full title: The Oxford Study Bible. Revised English Bible with the Apocrypha. Copyright 1992. Oxford University Press, Inc.)

Again, there are many excellent versions, such at the well-known *New International Version, King James Version, New Living Translation, New King James Version, English Standard Version, New Revised Standard Version, New American Bible,* and the *Living Bible.* Many other Bibles could be mentioned and added to this list.

In addition to using the REB for the majority of Jesus' quotes in this book, I also used with permission many quotes from the New American Standard Bible (NASB) Scripture taken from the NEW AMERICAN STANDARD BIBLE®, Copyright © 1960, 1962, 1963, 1968, 1971, 1972, 1973, 1975, 1995 by The Lockman Foundation, used by permission, and for a smaller number of Jesus' quotes, I used *The New Oxford Annotated Bible, Revised Standard Version* (RSV) (Copyright 1973. Oxford University Press). Thus, **when reading a quote in *Jesus Q* the reader should assume it is from the REB unless it is footnoted, or otherwise indicated,** in which case it is from the Revised Standard Version (RSV), New Revised Standard Version (NRSV), The New American Bible for Catholics (NAB), or The New Jerusalem Bible (NJB). Permission to quote from these Bibles is gratefully acknowledged.

I am grateful to Oxford University Press for granting permission for me to use these Bibles as sources for this book.

5. **Writing with insight about a holy man, who is the Son of God, is a supreme effort where mistakes are to be avoided at all costs.** There may be a few overlooked typographical errors in this book, which will be found and corrected. More important is the thought and reflection in *Jesus Q*, which I hope the reader finds beneficial.

The reader should not so much read *Jesus Q* as hear it.

Jesus said, "Happy are those who hear the word of God and keep it." Note Jesus did not say, "those who read the word of God." Why not? Because in his world, few Jews, Greeks, or Romans could read or write, so they heard news of their village, city, nation, and king, rather than read of it.

And you will also hear Jesus' wisdom as you read his questions.

The woman answered, "I know that Messiah (that is, Christ) is coming. When he comes he will make everything clear to us." Jesus said to her, "I am he, I who am speaking to you."

~ John 4:25-26

1 Why did you search for me?
Luke 2:49

They turned the city upside-down looking for their missing boy, but the parents didn't find a clue.

When they finally found him after three days, what did he ask his mother and father?

"Why did you search for me?" Luke 2:49

Luke's second chapter recounts the story:

> **When the festive season was over and they set off for home, the boy Jesus stayed behind in Jerusalem. His parents did not know of this; but supposing he was with the party they travelled for a whole day, and only then did they begin looking for him among their friends and relations. When they could not find him they returned to Jerusalem to look for him. Luke 2:43-45**

We can read Luke's story as a simple report of a young boy who was temporarily lost, but that view does not include a mother and father's love. So consider again the story while remembering his parents and you will find a powerfully emotional account.

But first read Luke's second chapter about young Jesus lost in Jerusalem, then return to read my own perceptions of Luke's report. This retelling is not in the Bible but it is based on a hundred walks I made through Jerusalem's Old City. It is inspired by what I saw and heard watching the young and old, Jew, Arab, and Gentile. It is also based upon the known archeology of what Jerusalem was like 2,000 years ago.

Here is my perspective based on my experience and the facts that Luke gives us.

Travelers in those days moved in long, slow caravans of donkeys, horses, and wagons to protect themselves from highway robbers, and so did the family of Jesus as they returned from their pilgrimage to Jerusalem, where they had just celebrated *Pesach*, called *Passover* in English. After a full day's journey back toward Nazareth, Mary and Joseph sought out Jesus, or as they would have said his name in Aramaic, *Yshua*. They thought he was on their caravan, but he wasn't. No one had seen him. No one knew where he was.

They rushed back to search for him – to Jerusalem – that great walled city of 250,000 inhabitants, thousands of pilgrims, and a garrisoned Roman army, because Jerusalem was a part of the Roman Empire.

But where in Jerusalem was Yshua? There were grim possibilities and one was especially dreadful: had their son been kidnapped and then sold into slavery like their ancestor Joseph had been? And if they found him as a slave, how much would the owner demand to sell him to his own parents? Would they have enough denarii – Rome's silver coins? They returned to the spot where their caravan had departed Jerusalem, but Jesus was not there. They returned to friends they had stayed with, but they had not seen him. They went to Jerusalem's noisy marketplace where thousands thronged, bargaining for vegetables, meat, leather sandals, tools, and knives. Joseph and Mary asked shopkeeper after shopkeeper if they had seen their boy. Many were sympathetic, others simply shrugged, a few rudely cut off their questions, and one short, bald man snapped, "Maybe you should keep a better eye on your boy." Others offered sincere but ultimately fruitless leads. Their boy was gone.

Joseph and Mary could not sleep that night and decided to walk Jerusalem's narrow, dark streets to the Roman garrison, to see if Jesus had been arrested. Their knock halted the loud, rough laughter from inside – the broad door suddenly swung open and a huge Roman Legionnaire – an iron gate of a man – stood just three feet away focusing his large, unblinking eyes on Mary and Joseph, holding them in his sight for several seconds, before he snorted Jesus was indeed under arrest, and abruptly spun around to retrieve him. Joseph was amazed a man so huge could move so fast. The Legionnaire returned with his shackled prisoner, who thrashed at his heavy, metal neckband like a wild animal. The Roman put his blazing torch-light tight to the prisoner's face, illuminating the bloody, rough features of an angry and muscular older teenager.

His Jesus was not their Jesus.

"Don't you recognize your own son!" the teenager yelled at Joseph with contempt, lurching so close to Joseph's face that he could feel the prisoner's breath. Although the prisoner was tall, he was still modest compared to the Roman, who kept a firm grip on his prisoner's chain, as though he was restraining an unruly dog. The Roman seemed pleased his Jesus was not the Jesus they sought, but he also saw the devastating sadness and disappointment in Mary and Joseph, who turned and slowly walked away. He watched them pensively for a moment before he shouted in a booming but reassuring voice, "You'll find your boy. He's probably just having a little fun someplace. Boys can be trouble – *I know* – I have three in Rome," his torch cast bright gold light on his wide smile and square teeth, but Joseph and Mary did not acknowledge his words and they turned a corner, heartbroken and despairing, into the unlit night.

After two days of searching, Jesus was nowhere to be found. Was he ill? Could he be near death? Did Mary and Joseph's nights pass in slow motion, waiting for morning to begin a new search? Joseph remembered his son's ready respect for adults, which should have reassured him, but as they could not find Jesus, it only magnified Joseph's concern. Mary recalled their family's happy earlier visits to Jerusalem, but Jesus had never been lost before.

On the third day they searched again, but now they were moving more slowly and with less direction. Joseph hid his fear in the shadows of the bright noon sun and when he took a sidelong glance at Mary, his heart broke to see her use the edge of her headscarf to dry her tears. The carpenter blinked hard, focused straight ahead, found her hand and squeezed her fingers tightly together, and at that moment, Joseph thought he heard Mary's words before she actually spoke, in a sort of pre-echo, "Let's go to the Temple and pray to God that we will find him in Jerusalem."

Walking up the massive staircase that led to the Temple, Mary and Joseph felt their steps slip into the smooth grooves worn into the stone steps from the thousands of worshippers who had climbed them before, even though the temple itself was not old, having been completed during Herod the Great's reign, not very many years before.

Mary remembered.

Twelve years earlier she had climbed this same staircase with her baby, holding his small head against her heart. Yshua was her child and God's miracle. She remembered him sleeping in her arms as she ascended the steps, undisturbed by the noisy multitudes. She remembered Joseph at her side, then as now. She remembered too the odd words that the Temple holy man Simeon had said to her 12 years ago, when he saw her holding the infant:

"This child is destined to be a sign that is rejected;
and you too will be pierced to the heart."
Luke 2:34-35

Is this what Simeon meant? She would lose her boy when he was 12-years-old? Was this her "pierced heart"? She prayed this was not what Simeon's words meant when he spoke with the Holy Spirit upon him.

Reaching the Temple mount, they heard hundreds of fellow Jews praying rhythmically in Aramaic, Hebrew, and Greek, each language layering on another, like a disjointed orchestra playing overlapping symphonies. Although Joseph could not see the altar, he caught the smell of burning sacrifices and stood momentarily hypnotized watching as white sacrificial smoke rose and lifted in front of the 15-story tall Temple. Joseph silently watched as the sacrificial smoke wove into a slow, twisting spiral and then disappeared into Jerusalem's bright blue sky.

Huge stone colonnades circled the court of the Temple casting gray shadows. In one of those shadows Mary noticed one especially large group loudly debating the prophets, and out of its many voices, a mother's astute hearing picked out her son's voice as it questioned the Pharisees. She instantly dropped her bags and ran toward the sound of her boy's voice, and when Joseph saw Mary running, he immediately ran after her.

The boy was seated. Yshua looked up at his mother and father, who were out of breath, and he smiled.

His parents were astonished to see him there, and his mother said to him, 'My son, why have you treated us like this? Your father and I have been anxiously searching for you.' 'Why did you search for me?' he said,
'Did you not know that I was bound to be in my Father's house?' But they did not understand what he meant."

Luke 2:48-50

Did you notice it? Something is said in Luke's story so shocking it has brought conflict to nations and the world, even to this day.

If you did not see it, don't worry; we will look at it very closely when it returns later.

> **2 Salt is good; but if the salt loses its saltiness, how will you season it?**
>
> **Mark 9:50**

Everyone will be salted with fire. Salt is good; but if the salt loses its saltiness, how will you season it? You must have salt within yourselves, and be at peace with one another.

Mark 9:49-50

Mark's parable is repeated in Matthew and Luke, with Luke's version adding,

Therefore, salt is good; but if even salt has become tasteless, with what will it be seasoned? It is useless

6

either for the soil or for the manure pile; it is thrown out. He who has ears, let him hear.
Luke 14:34-35 (NASB)

Salt is essential to life and if someone is deprived of salt they will become weak, suffer shock and go into a coma. So is this what Jesus warns us about – salt deficiency? No. Jesus is warning us about something more important than a nutritional deficiency.

The power of salt to preserve food became symbolic for the preservation and protection of a bond. So we can understand why the Greeks and Romans used salt in their pagan sacrifices, and why Israelites used salt in their sacrificial offerings. Salt symbolically says, "This will last, it is permanent."

We can read in Leviticus: "Every grain offering of yours, moreover, you shall season with salt, so that the salt of the covenant of your God shall not be lacking from your grain offering; with all your offering you shall offer salt." Leviticus 2:13 (NASB)

And in Numbers: "All the dedicated portions, which the Israelites set aside for the Lord, I give to you and to your sons and daughters with you as a due for all time. This is a perpetual covenant of salt before the Lord for you and your descendants also." Numbers 18:19

And this in Ezekiel: "When you have completed the purifying of the altar, you are to present a young bull without blemish and a ram without blemish. Present them before the Lord, and have the priests throw salt on them and sacrifice them as a whole-offering to the Lord." (43:23)

But wait, Jesus also said, "Everyone will be salted with fire." What can he mean?

Jesus refers to the Last Judgment. Paul wrote, "the day of judgment ... dawns in fire, and the fire will test the worth of each person's work.

7

(1 Cor. 2:13) And listen to the Baptist (Luke 3:16), "I baptize you with water; but there is one coming who is mightier than I am. … He will baptize you with the Holy Spirit and with fire." The Messiah said he came, "to set fire to the earth, and how I wish it were already kindled!" (Luke 12:49)

The actions of everyone will be judged by the Supreme Being when the ripples of every human act has caused its final effect and reached its ultimate destination.

The Messiah's words are hard – "I have come to set fire to the earth, and how I wish it were already kindled!" No followers of the Messiah can think of themselves as equal to the Messiah, or imagine that they themselves have come to bring fire to the earth, but the Son of God alone who has been anointed by the Father.

> **3 Is the lamp brought in to be put under the measuring bowl or under the bed?**
> **Mark 4:21**

Matthew's parable about salt is quickly followed by a parable on lamps, and Mark's Gospel turns it into a question:

> **"He said to them, 'Is the lamp brought in to be put under the measuring bowl or under the bed? No, it is put on the lampstand. Nothing is hidden, except to be disclosed, and nothing is concealed except to be brought into the open.'"**
> **Mark 4:21-22**

When the Bible speaks of light should we understand it only symbolically?

Consider the third sentence of Genesis:

Then God said, "Let there be light"; and there was light. Genesis 1:3 (NASB)

God, Jesus, and light are linked in the Bible.

David said, "The Lord is my light" (Psalms 27:1) and "by your light we are enlightened." (Psalms 36:9) Simeon saw the infant Jesus and called him "a light that will bring revelation to the Gentiles and glory to your people Israel." (Luke 2:32). Jesus himself said, "I am the light of the world. No follower of mine shall walk in darkness; he shall have the light of life." (John 8:12).

So, again the question: should we understand "light" in the Bible as only symbolic? No.

It was on a mountain accompanied by three disciples that Jesus' face "shone like the sun, and his clothes became a brilliant white." (Matthew 17:2) And we remember Paul's experience: "suddenly a light from the sky flashed all around him," as he fell to the ground and he heard the voice of Jesus. (Acts 9:3). Jews celebrate Hanukkah, the Feast of Lights, commemorating oil that burned for eight days, even though there was only enough oil to burn for one.

When we read of light in the Bible, we should understand it both literally and symbolically.

4 Woman, what concern is that to you and to me?

John 2:4 (NRSV)

And Jesus said to her, "Woman, what concern is that to you and to me? My hour has not yet come." John 2:4 (NRSV)

There are just three essential requirements to get a marriage license where I live near Washington, D.C.: First, one must be 18-years old, second, a license fee must be paid, and third, an authorized person must perform the ceremony, but witnesses are not required and the event can be put in order for $100.

But that is today and the Cana wedding story requires us to understand how weddings took place when Jesus lived in Israel.

During the time of Jesus, marriages in Israel were significant family events preceded by long negotiations between the families of the bride and groom. After the two families reached agreement and the wedding day was at hand, guests might travel long distances to attend the happy event. For the wedding at Cana, Jesus and Mary probably walked from Nazareth to Cana in one day, since Cana was nine miles north of Nazareth. They might have stopped to rest in Sepphoris, Galilee's largest city, which was located midpoint between their home in Nazareth and Cana.

Traveling the dusty roads to Cana, wedding guests would have carried a change of clothes, since wedding celebrations could last a week or longer, with the celebrations offering guests plenty to eat and to drink, with music, dancing, singing and good company.

It was at such a happy celebration that Mary told her son that their hosts had run out of wine for the wedding guests.

When Mary told Jesus about this shortage, which would have been embarrassing for the hosts, as well as the bride and groom, Jesus asked:

> **Woman, what concern is that to you and to me? My hour has not yet come.**
>
> **John 2:4 (NRSV)**

Despite his negative reply, Mary told the servants at the wedding to "Do whatever he tells you." (John 2:5). Jesus told servants to fill six jars with water. They did so and Jesus ordered them to take a sample of the "water" to the wedding's head steward for tasting, the head steward tasted and was amazed and went to the bridegroom, "Everyone serves the best wine first, and the poorer only when the guests have drunk freely; but you have kept the best wine till now." John 2:10

Jesus' changing water to wine provided a spectacular supply of wine for the wedding. Each of the six stone jars held 20-30 gallons, thus Jesus changed about 150 gallons of water into wine – an equivalent today of 757 standard bottles of wine.

You may be surprised to learn this simple story has four levels of awareness. The first level of awareness is the belief it happened; that is, that there was a wedding as described and Jesus and his mother attended it in Cana. The nonbeliever fails at this first step, and while admitting they were not there, and thus concede it *might* have happened, they say the Bible cannot be trusted to be historically accurate.

Another group failing at the first level of awareness are theologians who like to warn us not to read the Bible literally, especially concerning any reported Biblical miracles. This type of theologian distrusts the Bible and some of them spend entire academic careers in a kind of paralysis, painstakingly studying and debating the Bible; imagining the world has waited for centuries to hear them say the scriptures cannot be trusted.

We who believe John's Cana wedding report can advance to the second level of awareness, which requires us to reflect on Jesus' reaction to his mother's request.

When Jesus says to his mother: "Woman, what concern is that to you and to me?" adding that his hour had not yet come. Some say Jesus is referring to his final hour, his death.

I disagree. I think he was saying it was not yet the time to reveal his messianic powers.

Mary's reaction encourages us, for even though her son reacted indifferently to the news that their hosts had run out of wine, she nevertheless told servants, "Do whatever he tells you," *having faith he would help*, but perhaps she did *not know how he would help*, still, she tells servants to be ready. But hadn't Jesus told Mary it wasn't his time? Yes, he did, but this shows, I believe, that the Messiah will step out of time to answer calls for help.

The second level of awareness is recognizing Jesus' response to his mother's request.

The third level of awareness is an awareness of a miracle. While Mary and the servants are aware a miracle occurred, no one else noticed. New Testament critics dismiss it as a collection of stories written by people eager to show Jesus was a miracle worker. But if that is the case, isn't it odd that Jesus seems reluctant to perform a miracle? And then further strange that he then performs it in a way that keeps people from learning about it? The miracle of the wine at Cana remained unknown to the wedding guests – even as they drank the miracle wine.

If you had been a guest at this Cana wedding, what would you have seen? You would have known that Miriam and her son Yshua (as Mary and Jesus would have been called in their own language) were there. You probably would have been aware that Yshua was gaining a small reputation as a traveling teacher and rabbi. You probably would have enjoyed the wedding and perhaps spoken with some of Yshua's followers, and perhaps even Jesus himself. And you may have also noticed that there was an abundance of excellent wine and you may have thought that Miriam seemed particularly happy and proud of her son Jesus. But would you have known a miracle had occurred at Cana? Doubtful. If a miracle occurred in your life today, would you be aware of it?

So, the third level of awareness is an awareness of the miracle, and the fourth level is seeing the larger meaning of the Cana Wedding. To see the Cana miracle as simply relieving a wine shortage is less than what this story tells us – there is much more going on here. John does not use the word for miracle to describe what happened at Cana; instead, he uses the word for sign. But if it was a sign, what kind of a sign? Prophets saw it as a sign of the Kingdom of Heaven.

The prophet Amos 9:14 said:

> **I shall restore the fortunes of my people Israel;**
> **they will rebuild their devastated cities and live in**
> **them, plant vineyards and drink the wine.**

Isaiah 55:1 hints at Cana:

> **Come for water all who are thirsty;**
> **though you have no money, come, buy grain and eat;**
> **come, buy wine and milk, not for money, not for a price.**

And Proverbs 9:5 (NASB):

> **Come, eat of my food**
> **And drink of the wine I have mixed.**

Abundance accompanies the Kingdom of God and the Kingdom's bounty makes an early appearance at the Cana wedding through an unrecognized "sign."

This question makes me wonder: What is harder, to turn water to wine, or wine to blood?

5 What are you looking for?

John 1:38

When John the Baptist saw Jesus pass by him, the Baptist said, "Look, there is the lamb of God!" Two of the Baptist's disciples (Andrew was one), turned and began following Jesus, and when Jesus noticed them, he turned and asked, **"What are you looking for?"** (John 1:38)

"Rabbi, where are you staying?" Jesus said to come and see. The Gospel of John reports they did so and spent the remainder of the day with him. It must have been an incredible conversation because the first thing Andrew did after it was to find his brother Simon and tell him, "We have found the Messiah."

The question is simple: "What are you looking for?" but since it is Jesus who is asking, the question has eternal significance. And to those interested in following the Messiah, Jesus answers, "Come and see." And yet a little later in John, Jesus tells the religious leaders who doubted his mission: **You will look for me, but you will not find me; and where I am, you cannot come. (John 7:34)**

The Messiah invites those who are interested in him to follow him, but to those who doubt him, he says, "Where I am, you cannot come."

6 Do you believe because I told you that I saw you under the fig tree?

John 1:50

Do you believe because I told you that I saw you under the fig tree? You will see greater things than that.

John 1:50

Philip found Nathanael to tell him, "We have found the man of whom Moses wrote in the law, the man foretold by the prophets: it is Jesus, son of Joseph, from Nazareth." "Nazareth!" A surprised Nathanael replied. "Can anything good come from Nazareth?" Philip said, "Come and see." When Jesus saw Nathanael coming towards him, he said, "Here is an Israelite worthy of the name; there is nothing false in him." Nathanael asked him, "How is it you know me?" Jesus replied, "I saw you under the fig tree before Philip spoke to you." "Rabbi," said Nathanael, "you are the son of God; you are king of Israel." Jesus answered, "Do you believe this because I said I saw you under the fig tree? You will see greater things than that." Then he added, "In very truth I tell you all: you will see heaven wide open and God's angels ascending and descending upon the Son of Man." (John 1:45-51)

Early in his ministry Jesus tells Nathanael of his future glory; at the end of his ministry, when he was under arrest and the leaders asked if he is the Messiah, Jesus once again spoke about his future glory:

"I am," said Jesus; "and you will see the Son of Man seated at the right hand of the Almighty and coming with the clouds of heaven."

Mark 14:62

Nathanael is brought to awe when he hears of Jesus' future glory, but when religious leaders hear of it, they pronounce Jesus' death sentence. And so it is with the Word of God; many comprehend it with awe, but to those outside, the Word of God provokes hatred and even an urge to kill those who accept the Word of God as the Truth. To those who live by lies, Truth is a provocation.

The Sermon on the Mount | Questions 7-12 are from this sermon

In all the Roman Empire, three cities were supreme: *Athens* the center of sophisticated philosophy, *Jerusalem* with its Holy Temple and priests, and Imperial *Rome* itself, where Caesar ruled with majestic power over the tribes, peoples, and nations of Europe, the Middle East and Northern Africa.

We naturally assume any new and important teaching would have first been heard in these three cities, but that assumption would not be correct. The world's most important teaching was not first heard in Athens, Jerusalem or Rome, but on a countryside hill. Visitors to the traditional site of the Sermon on the Mount are sometimes disappointed to find a hill that does not compare to the Alps in beauty, the Rocky Mountains in grandeur, or the Blue Ridge Mountains in charm.

And since Jesus' teachings are meant for the entire world, shouldn't we expect Jesus to have taught in Jerusalem's theaters, amphitheaters, and hippodromes that could seat 7,000 to 14,000 people? But the Bible doesn't report Jesus teaching in any of those places. Why not? Was Jesus concerned that his followers might become violent if they had gathered in large numbers? Unlikely, his Jewish followers were peaceful, and besides, if Jesus was concerned about his followers getting together in large numbers, why did he permit large crowds to follow him? Such as the thousands who came to hear him teach for whom he multiplied fish and bread.

The Sermon on the Mount is the greatest teaching in history, yet Jesus didn't present it in the centers of government or in stadiums; instead, he taught it from a modest hill, and yet the power of this sermon and his teachings extends further than any other religion. It is fair to note that other religions tend to be highly concentrated in certain nations and among certain ethnic groups. Of the world's religions, Christianity can make the most authentic claim to be truly universal and to be the most widely accepted faith among all the nations, peoples, tribes, and tongues on earth.

Many Christians see Jesus' Sermon on the Mount as the heart of his teachings, and theologians have spent a lot of time trying to fit it into various structures – Social Gospel, eschatological viewpoints, etcetera. But we will consider it from the new perspective of the questions that Jesus asks in that famous Sermon.

The Sermon on the Mount is found in Matthew, chapters 5-7, with parallel elements of the Sermon dispersed throughout Luke's Gospel, where it is known as the Sermon on the Plain.

Reader please note: the next six questions – numbers 7 through 12 – are a group of questions belonging to the Sermon on the Mount / Sermon on the Plain.

> **7 If you love only those who love you, what credit is that to you? Even sinners love those who love them. Again, if you do good only to those who do good to you, what credit is there in that?**
>
> **Luke 6:32-33**

If you love only those who love you, what credit is that to you? Even sinners love those who love them. Again, if you do good only to those who do good to you, what credit is there in that? Even sinners do as much. And if you lend only where you expect to be repaid, what credit is there in that? Even sinners lend to each other to be repaid in full.

Luke 6:32-34

Matthew 5:46 parallels Luke, above.

Humans welcome in order that they might be welcomed in return and lend to receive in return, hopefully with interest, but the Master asks, what reward should be expected for living life for our own direct, personal advantage, and he taught the following rule:

But love your enemies, and do good, and lend, expecting nothing in return; and your reward will be great, and you will be sons of the Most High; for He Himself is kind to the ungrateful and evil *men*. Be merciful, just as your Father is merciful.

Luke 6:35-36 (NASB)

This radical teaching advocates setting aside the leading principle of all social, business, political transactions – the principle of reciprocity. Human relations are built on reciprocity, whether one is buying groceries or nations are signing trade agreements, equal value and fair exchange are expected. While reciprocity is common sense, the Messiah taught that our common-sense expectations should not apply to everything we do. He wants us to *reconsider* reciprocity and to think of it in a *new* way.

The Messiah's followers should not expect reciprocity with humans, but rather reciprocity granted by God. Followers of the Messiah now have, in a sense, a reciprocal agreement with God, and because He grants blessings to all without conditions, we are required to reciprocally grant to others without conditions.

Jesus lived in a rigid eye-for-an-eye and tooth-for-a-tooth world. Jesus saw this balance sheet reality and taught a new standard where his followers must imitate God and so become sons of God.

> **"There must be no limit to your goodness, as your heavenly Father's goodness knows no bounds."**
> **Matthew 5:48**

No limits to one's goodness? Absurd! Shouldn't a religion be based upon what is realistic? Does any religious teaching equal this impossible appeal for goodness without limits? Does any philosophy or ideology present a more difficult challenge? This is a revolutionary and radical teaching.

> **8 Are you not worth more than the birds? Can anxious thoughts add a single day to your life? And why be anxious about clothes?**
>
> **Matthew 6:26-28**

Look at the birds in the sky; they do not sow and reap and store in barns, yet your heavenly Father feeds them. Are you not worth more than the birds? Can anxious thoughts add a single day to your life? And why be anxious about clothes? Consider how lilies grow in the fields; they do not work, they do not spin; yet I tell you, even Solomon in all his splendour was not attired like one of them. If that is how God clothes the grass in the fields, which is there today and tomorrow is thrown on the stove, will he not all the more clothe you? How little faith you have! Do not ask anxiously, "What are we to eat? What are we to drink? What shall we wear?" These are things that occupy the minds of the heathen, but your heavenly Father knows that you need them all. Set your mind on God's kingdom and his justice before everything else, and all the rest will come to you as well.

Matthew 6:26-33

Our world values money, but Jesus asks this striking question about value and worth, *"Are you not worth more than the birds?"*

His question contradicts the materialist's view that humans are not superior to apes or other animals. I remember a report of a gunman taking hostages at a television channel's corporate offices and making demands they broadcast a "commitment to save the planet." The gunman called civilization's religious roots "disgusting" and says nothing is more important than saving "The Lions, Tigers, Giraffes, Elephants, Froggies, Turtles, Apes, Raccoons, Beetles, Ants, Sharks, Bears, and of course, the Squirrels." The hostage-taker hated humans, calling children the "future catastrophic pollution" and "their parents are the current pollution." The man pronounced: "No more babies."[1]

Few environmentalists are this mad, and in actual fact, we know many environmentalists do fine work. Yet, today, it is true millions of people are confused about the place of humans in the natural hierarchy – or if there even is a natural hierarchy. Jesus teaches a God-created order – a hierarchy. God created birds and values them so much as part of His creation, that Jesus taught God's aware if a small finch dies. But he also taught that the value of a human surpasses that of an animal.

Are you not worth more than the birds?
Matthew 6:26

His question brings us back to the Truth: God created an ordered universe, a hierarchy where one thing is of greater value than something else. We know this in our material world, which is why we always want to know what something costs. But Jesus isn't talking about value established by money, but value established by God.

If you understand the truth in this question of Jesus – **Are you not worth more than the birds?** – you will avoid many errors in popular culture.

As the Creator of all, God understands the value of everything. Jesus tells us there is a cosmic order and men and women rank higher than animals because men and women are *made in the image of God.* These

---

[1] The Washington Post, September 2, 2010, Section A

words sometimes trigger a mocking response from anti-Christians, who reply: "Image of God! What does that mean? God has a body? God has two arms and two legs? He's a bearded old man?"

That is misguided thinking. Being made in the image of God means we are in some way like Him. With our reason and reading the Hebrew and Christian Testaments, we can sense the outline of that likeness.

God created distinctions between humans and animals, a dividing line between humans and animals. We do not know with total precision what it is, but the fact that men and women can know truth through reason and faith, and animals cannot, is a primary distinction. Having a human soul is another. If someone does not believe the truth of Genesis or the words of Jesus of Nazareth, they are unlikely to accept the truth about a created natural order, or to believe that they are created in the "image of God."

But understand something. If you acknowledge the God of Israel as creator of all reality, then you will logically acknowledge He deserves honor, praise, and reverence from His creation. With that acknowledgement inevitably comes an understanding that He requires us to love and respect His creation, including animals, and most especially, other humans. Love of God leads to love of humans and His creation.

Also understand this. If you doubt the existence of God and His creation of a natural order, it is likely that you will eventually adopt some peculiar beliefs. Then frequently, over time, sometimes months, sometimes years, mental turmoil may result, and your doubts and disbelief will cause you to begin hating the idea of God, and inevitably, cause you to hate what He made in His image, other humans.

When someone rejects God's Truth, they think they do not need to answer to anyone or anything. One eminent Christian leader put it this way: "When there is no God, there is no morality and, in fact, no mankind either."[2]

Q 8 continued

> **And which of you by worrying can add a *single* hour to his life's span?**
> **If then you cannot do even a very little thing, why do you worry about other matters?**
> **Luke 12:25-26 (NASB)**

> **Do not be afraid, little flock, for your Father has chosen gladly to give you the kingdom.**
> **Luke 12:32 (NASB)**

Anxiety is common. Gloom rolls in on our digital devices with downbeat economic news, increasing political hostility, and large-scale natural disasters. Constantly connected to the Internet means constantly connected to news, and much of it is unhappy.

But anxiety is not what God intends for his followers. The man from Nazareth tells us to maintain certainty in God and leave tomorrow's problems for tomorrow.

Let's reflect on what anxiety is. Psychologists classify five basic emotions: happiness, sadness, disgust, anger, and fear. Of these basic emotions, fear is related to anxiety, but differs because fear is focused, while anxiety is vague. Anxiety is doubt about what the next week, day, or hour might bring. Fear faces us from the front, while anxiety stands behind us and whispers, "You better worry – this could go badly."

Jesus was human and understood anxiety. We know how he reacted when he saw anxiety in friends, as he said to Martha, "Martha, Martha,

---

[2] The National Catholic Bioethics Center. *On Conscience, Two Essays by Cardinal Joseph Ratzinger*, (Ignatius Press, Philadelphia, 2007)

you are worried and bothered about so many things; but *only* one thing is necessary, for Mary has chosen the good part which shall not be taken away from her." (Luke 10:41-42 NASB) When the disciples became anxious about feeding 5,000, Jesus tweaked their anxiety by saying, "Give them something to eat yourselves." Shocked, they said, "All we have here,' they said, 'is five loaves and two fish.'" (Matthew 14:17) "Where are we to buy bread to feed these people?" (John 6:5)

Yet Jesus said do not be anxious or worry. Then what about fear?

Envision yourself on a peaceful forest path walking among green trees that surround and shade you from the bright sunlight. The air is light and you can hear bluebirds and robins, and you smell the pines as trees throw shadows onto your path – when a brown bear suddenly ambles in front of you. It is huge and in a bad mood – it looks straight at you and growls. You do not experience vague anxiety; you feel fear. Jesus didn't say have no fear of danger; rather, he said do not be anxious with vague doubts.

You may think, "Well, if fear is okay in some circumstances, why does Jesus say in Luke? **'Do not be afraid, little flock, for your Father has chosen gladly to give you the kingdom.' Luke 12:32 (NASB)** Or why does David say in the Psalms 23:4, **'Even were I to walk through a valley of deepest darkness I should fear no harm, for you are with me,'** or what about 1 John 4:18, **'In love there is no room for fear; indeed perfect love banishes fear. For fear has to do with punishment, and anyone who is afraid has not attained to love in its perfection.'** Doesn't each of these passages counsel against fear?"

Each of these verses addresses a specific fear: a fear of death when Jesus of Nazareth promised life, a fear of punishment after God has pardoned, or fear of not gaining the Kingdom of Heaven when God promises it to His followers. That said, the question about fear remains an important one: Should Christians fear?

Moses said this about fear, telling Israelite judges:

You must be impartial and listen to high and low alike: have no fear of your fellows, for judgment belongs to God.

Deuteronomy 1:17

When the Israelites prepared to enter the Promised Land, they became discouraged after learning they would face a people who lived in a fortified land, yet Moses warned Israelites against fear.

You must not dread them or be afraid. The Lord your God who goes at your head, will fight for you; he will do again what you saw him do for you in Egypt and in the wilderness.

Deuteronomy 1:29-31

And here is Moses again: **"You are to fear the Lord your God"** and to serve him alone (Deuteronomy 6:13), in addition, God told Moses to tell the Israelites:

You must not victimize one another, but fear your God, because I am the Lord your God. Observe my statutes, keep my judgements, and carry them out; and you will live without any fear in the land.

Leviticus 25:17-18

Searching the Bible for the word "fear" one sees many references, particularly in the Old Testament. These "fear" passages in both the Old and New Testaments are best understood in four categories.

First things first: fear, revere and honor the Creator.

Let the whole earth fear the Lord and all earth's inhabitants stand in awe of him. For he spoke, and it was; he commanded, and there it stood.

Psalm 33:8

Second: the Bible tells us not to fear man and woman, which is to say: fear the Creator not the created.

> **Fear of men may prove a snare, but trust in the Lord is a tower of refuge.**
>
> **Proverbs 29:25**

> **The Lord is my light and my salvation; whom should I fear?**
>
> **Psalm 27:1**

Third aspect to understanding fear: the fear of God is for our good, our blessings, our security and future.

> **Those who fear the Lord trust in the Lord: he is their help and their shield.**
>
> **Psalm 115:11**

> **The Lord confides his purposes to those who fear him; his covenant is for their instruction.**
>
> **Psalm 25:14**

> **News of misfortune will have no terrors for him, because his heart is steadfast, trusting in the Lord. His confidence is well established, he has no fears, and in the end he will see the downfall of his enemies.**
>
> **Psalm 112:7-8**

The fourth category to understanding fear unravels what fear of the Lord *means*. Proverbs tells us.

> **The fear of the Lord is the foundation of knowledge; it is fools who scorn wisdom and instruction.**
>
> **Proverbs 1:7**

> **The fear of the Lord is to hate evil;**
> **Pride and arrogance and the evil way**
> **And the perverted mouth, I hate.**
> **Proverbs 8:13 (NASB)**

Now we can understand fear as God wants it understood. *Fear of the Lord* is *the foundation of knowledge* and to hate evil. Many in the "Culture of Death," as Pope John Paul II called it, are confused about what evil is, but Proverbs (8:13) reminds us it is: pride, arrogance, the evil way, and perverted talk.

Now our knowledge of fear is on the right track: fear of God is hatred of evil, and fear of God is the foundation of knowledge, and we also know Psalm 111 says fear of the Lord is *only the beginning* of wisdom.

> **The fear of the Lord is the beginning of wisdom,**
> **and they who live by it grow in understanding.**
> **Psalm 111:10**

The fear of a Holy God frees humans from all fears, and so spoke Zechariah, the father of John the Baptist, with the power of the Holy Spirit.

> **To grant us that we, being rescued from the hand**
> **of our enemies,**
> **Might serve Him without fear**
> **Luke 1:74 (NASB)**

And so spoke David in the Psalms:

> **I sought the Lord, and He answered me,**
> **And delivered me from all my fears**
> **Psalm 34:4 (NASB)**

Now we see more clearly what "fear of the Lord" means.

Jesus is clear about whom to fear.

> **To you who are my friends I say: do not fear those who kill the body and after that have nothing more they can do. I will show you whom to fear: fear him who, after he has killed, has authority to cast in hell. Believe me, he is the one to fear.**
>
> **Luke 12:4-5**

We finish our consideration of fear with the book of Revelation (15:2), where John sees "those who had been victorious against the beast, its image, and the number of its name," singing:

> **Great and marvellous are your deeds,**
> **O Lord God, sovereign over all;**
> **just and true are your ways,**
> **O King of the ages.**
> **Who shall not fear you, Lord,**
> **and do homage to your name?**
> **For you alone are holy.**
> **All nations shall come and worship**
> **before you, for your just decrees stand revealed.**
>
> **Revelation 15:3-4**

Continuing with questions Jesus asked in his Sermon on the Mount, where he posed a stream of Qs in Luke and Matthew (chapters 6 and 7, respectively).

9 Can one blind man guide another? Will not both fall into the ditch?

Luke 6:39

Jesus' Q in Luke 6:39 and Matthew 7:3 are closely associated so we will consider them both as Q 9.

Why do you look at the speck that is in your brother's eye, but do not notice the log that is in your own eye?

Matthew 7:3 (NASB)

10 Would any of you offer your son a stone when he asks for bread, or a snake when he asks for a fish? If you, bad as you are, know how to give good things to your children, how much more will your heavenly Father give good things to those who ask him!

Matthew 7:9-11

> 11 You will know them by your fruits. Grapes are not gathered from thorn *bushes* nor figs from thistles, are they?
>
> Matthew 7:16 (NASB)

> 12 a When the day comes, many will say to me, "Lord, Lord, did we not prophesy in your name, drive out demons in your name, and in your name perform many miracles?" Then I will tell them plainly, "I never knew you. Out of my sight, your deeds are evil!"
>
> Matthew 7:22-23

> 12 b Why do you call Me, 'Lord, Lord,' and do not do what I say?
>
> Luke 6:46 (NASB)

Frightful images of blind people being led into pits by other blind people, of starving children given rocks to eat, eyes blinded by wooden boards, vicious wolves disguised as sheep, and then a baffling image of miracle workers and prophets ordered into hell.

At first glance, these questions in Q9-12 do not seem to be related, but they are; each is about human sight.

"Can a blind person guide a blind person?" Obviously, no, but reality is more subtle. Let's reconsider. Blindness varies in cause and degree; in one case it can be the complete loss of vision, in another case it is limited to one eye, or it may only mean night blindness. Causes of blindness can be neurological or psychogenic, such as hysterical blindness, which does not result from biological malfunction, but from a mental or psychic inability to see. Here the Master is using the condition of blindness to teach us about a different type of blindness – perceptual blindness – a blindness to truth.

> **Can one blind man guide another? Will not both fall into the ditch?**
>
> **Luke 6:39**

In a related Sermon on the Mount question (Q9) Jesus calls the educated scribes and Pharisees blind who do not see the more important aspects of the law such as good faith. Pharisees are not only unaware of their blindness, but lead others into darkness.

In the second question in this group Jesus denounces blindness caused by hypocrisy,

> **Why do you look at the speck of sawdust in your brother's eye, with never a thought for the plank in your own? How can you say to your brother, 'Let me take the speck out of your eye,' while all the time there is a plank in your own?**
>
> **Matthew 7:3-4**

Hypocrisy deforms the eyesight, causing blindness in those who focus on the flaws of others while unaware of their own shortcomings.

Q10 in this Q9-12 grouping:

Would any of you offer your son a stone when he asks for bread, or a snake when he asks for a fish? If you, bad as you are, know how to give good things to your children, how much more will your heavenly Father give good things to those who ask him!

Matthew 7:9-11

Again, sight is at issue. If even terrible people see their children's needs and meet them, then of course God sees our needs and fulfills them, including our wishes, if they will ultimately bring happiness.

Q11 is again, metaphorically, about "sight" and using "sight" to see the truth about leaders.

You will know them by their fruits. Grapes are not gathered from thorn *bushes* nor figs from thistles, are they? So every good tree bears good fruit, but the bad tree bears bad fruit.

Matthew 7:16-17 (NASB)

Jesus tells us how to see false prophets and deceitful leaders: do their words match what they produce? Do their pledges of peace match the wars they start? Do their claims to respect Christians harmonize with the actions they take that offend Christian conscience and Biblical teaching? *Watch what they actually do, not their speeches or sermons.* Do their teachings increase Biblical understanding or only increase understanding of their own philosophy?

The 12th question is again about sight, but from a different perspective.

Not everyone who says to me, 'Lord, Lord,' will enter the kingdom of heaven, but only those who do the will of my heavenly Father. When the day comes, many will say to me, 'Lord, Lord, did we

not prophesy in your name, drive our demons
in your name, and in your name perform many
miracles?' Then I will tell them plainly, 'I never
knew you. Out of my sight, your deeds are evil!'
Matthew 7:21-23

This time Scripture is talking about God's perfect sight, as we read
in Proverbs (15:3 NASB), "The eyes of the Lord are in every place,
Watching the evil and the good."

Jesus says when Judgment comes many will claim they have spoken
prophecies in his name and also conducted exorcisms and miracles.
Even so, in some cases, all of their works will prove insufficient, as
Proverbs (16:2 NASB) says: "All the ways of a man are clean in his
own sight, But the Lord weighs the motives."

"Why do you call me, 'Lord, Lord' – and never do what I tell you?"
Jesus asks in Luke (6:46), and Matthew expands the statement, **"Not
everyone who says to me, 'Lord, Lord' will enter the kingdom of
Heaven, but only those who do the will of my heavenly Father."
Matthew 7:21**

We know actions surpass words from Isaiah, James, and Romans:

> **Because this people worship me with empty words
> and pay me lip-service while their hearts are far
> from me, and their religion is but a human precept,
> learned by rote.**
>
> **Isaiah 29:13**

> **But prove yourselves doers the word, and not
> merely hearers who delude themselves.**
>
> **James 1:22 (NASB)**

> **None will be justified before God by hearing the
> law, but by doing it.**
>
> **Romans 2:13**

All the questions in this group (9-12) use physical sight as an analogy for spiritual sight. Spiritual blindness prevents us from seeing the truth about others and ourselves.

The Creator has perfect insight into human actions and motivations. The Psalmist said, "He who planted the ear, does He not hear? He who formed the eye, does He not see? **(94:9 NASB)**

Sight and blindness are not secondary issues to Jesus – they are primary reasons the Messiah came into the world. Listen to his words in John:

> **Jesus said, 'It is for judgement that I have come into this world – to give sight to the sightless and to make blind those who see.' Some Pharisees who were present asked, 'Do you mean that we are blind?' 'If you were blind,' Jesus said, 'you would not be guilty, but because you claim to see, your guilt remains.'**
> **John 9:39-41**

13 If you do not believe me when I talk to you about earthly things, how are you to believe if I should talk about the things of heaven?

John 3:12

Nicodemus is an educated Pharisee and member of the Sanhedrin – the Jewish Council – and he heard Jesus teaching the crowds and he found his words to be profound, and Nicodemus wants to know more about this rabbi from Nazareth. He wants to ask the rabbi questions, but he's afraid to visit him in public, because while some Pharisees admire Jesus, many others distrust him. These skeptical Pharisees wonder where Jesus was educated, who taught him, and what is the source of his miraculous powers.

Nicodemus hides his curiosity about Jesus from the other Pharisees and waits until after nightfall to seek out and talk with the man from Nazareth. Jesus tells the curious Nicodemus, "Truly, truly, I say to you, unless one is born again he cannot see the kingdom of God." (John 3:3 NASB) Strange words, which cause Nicodemus to reply, "How can a man be born when he is old? He cannot enter a second time into his mother's womb and be born, can he?" (John 3:4 NASB)

Jesus seems surprised that Nicodemus, an educated man, cannot grasp his meaning, "Are you the teacher of Israel and do not understand these things?" (John 3:10 NASB)

If you do not believe me when I talk to you about earthly things, how are you to believe if I should talk about the things of heaven?

John 3:12

Jesus uses human birth to teach about spiritual rebirth. He uses what is known and visible to teach what is enigmatic and invisible. A newborn is a new creation and only new creations can see the Kingdom of Heaven. Jesus clarifies his words for Nicodemus: "Flesh can give birth only to flesh; it is spirit that gives birth to spirit." Also notice that Jesus' question to Nicodemus uses the word "believe" twice: "If you do not believe ... how are you to believe ...?" Believing is key.

Did Nicodemus begin to believe and then to understand, or did he begin to understand and then to believe?

14 Where are they? Has no one condemned you?

John 8:10

We know the story: a woman is caught in adultery, arrested, and brought by the scribes and Pharisees to Jesus to test his loyalty to the Law, which called for her to be stoned to death. The woman's accusers question Jesus about the appropriate punishment for her, but he doesn't reply, instead he bends down and writes in the dirt with his finger, then, standing up, tells her accusers that the one without guilt should begin her death sentence and throw the first rock.

The innocent person in this story who could justly judge this woman is Jesus, but he does not. All of the accusers retreat after Jesus poses his question. Jesus then asks the accused, **"Where are they? Has no one condemned you?"** She responds, "No one, sir." "Neither do I condemn you," Jesus said. "Go; do not sin again." (John 8:10-11)

This story frequently brings two reactions: one is awe at Jesus' compassionate response to a life-or-death situation; the other is relief that this story is about someone in the distant past. But the story could be about us and the future.

To understand this possibility, remember that the Bible calls Satan our accuser. Revelation says Satan accuses Christians day and night before God. The Old Testament tells the story of Satan accusing Job before God, with Satan telling God that Job only honors Him because of the great wealth God had given to Job. In response, God grants Satan the power to test Job by destroying Job's property, and after additional accusations by Satan, grants Satan the power to further test Job by taking away Job's health.

Some religious traditions believe that when we stand for judgment after death, Satan will be there with an excellent memory and persuasive power to accuse us of every wrong we have ever committed. But the Christian will say to Jesus, these accusations are true, but after accepting the Good News I became a follower and I lived by what you taught. Satan will leave defeated, and Jesus will ask the Christian, as he asked the woman in the story, where are your accusers, and the Christian will answer, "There are none, Sir," and the Master will say, "Then the King will say to those on His right, 'Come, you who are blessed of My Father, inherit the kingdom prepared for you from the foundation of the world.'" (Matthew 25:34 NASB)

It is possible we are the woman in this story who will be brought for judgment by our accusers, who will argue we deserve the full penalty of the law – eternal death, but Jesus will reward anyone who hears the Word of God and acts on it. That is the Good News.

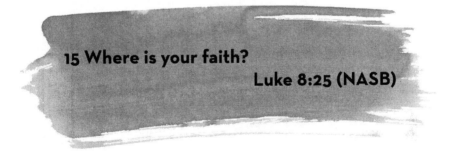

15 Where is your faith?
Luke 8:25 (NASB)

Luke wrote about Jesus and his disciples caught in a storm. We wonder what it was like? What was it like to be on a rocking boat with Jesus and the twelve when the storm hit? In my mind's eye, it may have been something like this.

The twelve men had been rowing and talking amongst themselves when strong wind, rain, and darkness descended over them and quickly pushed them into a life-or-death fight, as their boat pitched and rolled beyond their collective strength to control it.

The storm tossed Matthew overboard as he clung to the side yelling for help, Peter rushes to him and grabs Matthew's hands to pull him back on board, but instead, Peter finds himself drawn towards a sinking Matthew and the dark sea. Thomas rushes to both of them, encircles his arms around Peter's waist from behind, and successfully yanks both Peter and Matthew back onto the rocking, jolting boat. The others were completely terrified by the black clouds and the hard, stinging rain. Peter yells so loud everyone hears him, even over the onslaught of the wind: "Where's the Master?" "He's asleep!" John yells back. "What!" Peter says in shock, and looks where John points, to someone bundled in a thick, brown blanket, asleep on a pillow at the back of the boat. The wind is becoming more savage and their boat is flooding. Peter shouts to John to wake Jesus, as John is nearest to their leader. Slipping and falling, John makes his way to Jesus, grasps his blanket, which did not seem to be soaked with rain, but he is too panicked to wonder at this, and he pulls the blanket down from Jesus' head and shakes him, screaming, "Master, don't you care! We are drowning!" Jesus did not seem annoyed at being woken, but rather at John's woeful fear. Jesus stands and orders the winds and sea to calm, and then he asks, "Why are you such cowards? How little faith you have!" (Matthew 8:26)

There is mutual astonishment: the disciples are astonished their leader slept as they were drowning and Jesus is astonished that his men panicked.

The calming of the storm is reported in both Matthew and Luke, although the question Jesus asks varies a little in each. In Matthew 8:26 (NASB) Jesus asked: **"Why are you afraid, you men of little faith?** In Luke it is: **"Where is your faith?" (Luke 8:25 NASB)** His question can also be understood as, "Where is your trust?" or "Where is your confidence?"

Some may think the Messiah's criticism of his men to be a bit unfair; after all, their boat was flooding, and they thought they would soon die in a violent storm.

But Jesus was a rabbi and rabbis teach, so it is possible that only a few hours earlier that very day, Jesus had taught his disciples David's 46th Psalm,

> **"God is our refuge and our stronghold, a timely help in trouble; so we are not afraid though the earth shakes and the mountains move in the depths of the sea, when its waters seethe in tumult."**
>
> **Psalm 46:1-3**

If this was the case, then Jesus' question, **"Where is your faith?"** seems very reasonable. Perhaps only a few hours earlier, Jesus has told his men to maintain courage and trust in God when "waters seethe in tumult."

But just a short time later, his men panicked in rough waters.

"Where is your faith?" – Jesus of Nazareth

16 Why do you harbour these thoughts? Is it easier to say, "Your sins are forgiven you," or to say, "Stand up and walk"?
Luke 5:22-23

Matthew, Mark, and Luke write of a paralyzed man whose friends were determined to bring him to the miracle-worker from Nazareth. That was a challenge because it meant getting their handicapped friend through huge crowds that surrounded Jesus. They had a plan: they would get their immobile friend to Jesus by cutting a hole in the roof of the home where Jesus was teaching, and then lower him down to Jesus on a stretcher. They accomplished their plan and Jesus was so impressed with their faith, he said to the crippled man, "Your sins are forgiven you." (Luke 5:20) When Jewish leaders heard this they thought that Jesus spoke irreverently, because only God can forgive sins. Jesus knew what they were thinking and said to them, **"Why do you harbour these thoughts? Is it easier to say, 'Your sins are forgiven you,' or to say, 'Stand up and walk'? But to convince you that the Son of Man has the right on earth to forgive sins"** – he turned to the paralyzed man – **"I say to you, stand up, take your bed, and go home."** (Luke 5:22-24, also see Matthew 9:5 and Mark 2:9)

The Messiah responds to the faith of the paralyzed man and his friends by first forgiving sins, and second, by a physical healing. This is an unusual response by Jesus. Why? Because when Jesus encountered doubt by religious leaders, he usually left them in their doubts. This time, however, he grants a visible lesson that Israel's God has given him power to forgive sins and verifies this by a miraculous healing.

> "They were all lost in amazement and praised God; filled with awe they said, 'The things we have seen today are beyond belief!'" – Scribes and Pharisees
> (Luke 5:26)

17 Can you make the bridegroom's friends fast while the bridegroom is with them?
Luke 5:34

Pharisees and scribes want to know about the habits and conduct of Jesus' disciples, whose eating and drinking compares unfavorably with the Baptist's disciples, who were renown for prayerfulness and fasting.

> **Jesus replied, 'Can you make the bridegroom's friends fast while the bridegroom is with them? But the time will come when the bridegroom will be taken away from them; that will be the time for them to fast.**
> **Luke 5:34-35 (also Matthew 9:15 and Mark 2:19)**

Jesus' answer recalls the famous verse in Ecclesiastes (3:1-4)

> For everything its season, and for every activity its time: a time to be born and a time to die; a time to plant and a time to uproot; a time to kill and a time to heal; a time to break down and a time to build up; a time to weep and a time to laugh; a time for mourning and a time for dancing.

Reader please note: We'll consider Question 18 and Question 19 (19 a and 19 b) together as they are very closely related. Question 19 a and 19 b are in my view essentially the same. So let's consider the heart of questions.

18 Do you believe that I have the power to do what you want?
Matthew 9:28

and Jesus asked, "Do you believe that I have the power to do what you want?" "We do," they said.

Then he touched their eyes, and said, "As you have believed, so let it be"; and their sight was restored.
Matthew 9:28-30

19 a Jesus found him and asked, "Have you faith in the Son of Man?"

John 9:35

19 b Jesus said, "I am the resurrection and the life. Whoever has faith in me shall live, even though he dies; and no one who lives and has faith in me shall ever die. Do you believe this?"

John 11:25-26

All of these questions are about faith:

> "*Do you believe* I have the power to do what you want?"

> "*Have you faith* in the Son of Man?"

> "*Whoever has faith* in me shall live, even though he dies."

The italics are mine.

Is the call for faith only difficult or is it impossible? Nonbelievers say faith is impossible and call Jesus' claims unreasonable and unproven. And yet the nonbelievers *do believe...* it's just that *they don't believe Jesus' claims are true.*

> He claims he is the way and the truth and the life.

> He claims he is the one called the anointed, the Messiah, the Son of God.

> He claims that whoever believes in him, even if he dies, will live.

> He claims that no one comes to the Father except through Jesus.

> And even more difficult for many to believe is his claims that, "In very truth I tell you, before Abraham was born, I am."

Some people want proof before they accept Jesus is who he says he is. Yet, these same people make decisions on faith every day.

I will explain, but first let's agree on what the word "faith" means. We will use the dictionary's definition – *faith* is belief, complete trust, or confidence in someone or something. Using this definition, modest faith is necessary to conduct a business transaction with a friend; but more faith is needed to conduct one with a stranger.

Less faith and trust is needed to buy a car from a close relative; but more faith is needed to buy a car from an unfamiliar used-car dealer.

Less faith and trust is necessary to marry someone you have known since childhood, but more faith is necessary to marry someone you met last month on the internet.

Some might challenge: "Of course we make some decisions on faith or trust – but it is not the most desirable way to make decisions. We should try to reduce those kinds of decisions and understand all the relevant factors before deciding on a course of action, and thus make decisions based more on logic and reason, to the degree that it is possible, and less on faith or trust."

Okay, fine, so let's think about the daring line of work of being an astronaut, which is certainly a logic-based occupation. Every assignment an astronaut undertakes during a mission is carefully planned in advance. There is no guesswork, faith, or trust. It is all physics, mathematics, chemistry, electronics, metallurgy, and biology. Agree? But consider this: what astronaut travels into space if they did not trust in the hundreds of scientists and engineers who planned their mission? Would an astronaut travel into space without trust in those who designed the rocket, the spacesuit they wear, and trust in the thousands of machinists who built their spacecraft, precision part-by-precision part? No, they would not. Without trust in the humans who built the spacecraft and faith in their calculations, without that trust, no astronaut would ever sit atop a rocket waiting for launch. But they do go – because they have confidence (trust and belief) in the engineers and scientists who planned their mission to orbit the Earth at 18,000 miles per hour.

"Yes and that's why I would never want to be an astronaut," some might think.

Then what about that jet flight you will take? Are you comfortable with the FAA's safety protocols? Do you trust that airline's maintenance staff? Do you have faith that they will ensure the jet engines are perfectly maintained? Do you trust the airline's safety record? Do you think the airport's security team will adequately check the passengers? What about the pilot? Do you know him or her? Do you know *anyone* who knows the pilot? *Do you know anything at all about the pilot?*

I remember a plane crash where it was determined that the cause of the crash was: "lack of discipline and excessive self-assurance" of the pilot, co-pilot, and flight engineer – the pilot had a blood-alcohol level that would have made it illegal for him to drive a car in the United States.[3]

You see my point. Even astronauts in a highly controlled profession take much on trust, which is to say on faith. Jet passengers also take a great deal on faith. Even automobile drivers have faith in the cars they drive and about other drivers on the road, those strangers about whom drivers knows nothing as they travel on roads to their destinations.

Does something connect the faith and trust of astronauts to the faith and trust of Christians? Yes! Both base their faith and trust on testimony! For astronauts it is their trust in the testimony of engineers and scientists, it is trust in their statements, and in their records of telling the truth. In the case of jet passengers, it is trust and faith based on the testimony of what they have read, heard, and know about the airline, and on their own experience with it. In the case of Christians, it is trust in the testimony of the prophets and the apostles. Trust in the testimony of those who wrote the New Testament; those writers who knew Jesus personally, or who knew people who knew Jesus personally. Or perhaps those who lived not very long after Jesus had lived and knew people who had personally seen and heard Jesus of Nazareth.

We *all* live our lives on what we believe to be truthful testimony. *All of us.* Astronauts – airlines passengers – everyone lives faith-based lives, making faith-based decisions. *We all live by faith in the testimony of those we have chosen to trust.* We all live faith-based lives. It is just that not all of us admit that fact… *the fact of faith.*

I suspect someone, perhaps an agnostic, will read this and say they have neither faith, nor disbelief in God, and they object to my saying we all lead faith-based lives. Such an individual might say:

---

[3] The Wall Street Journal, 9-20-2011, internet

Nice attempt, but please do not equate accepting the laws of physics, or air travel, or space travel, or a surgeon performing an operation, with accepting Bible stories about walking on water and magically multiplying bread. That first type of trust is based on established science; the Christian type of trust is based upon Bible stories. We are talking about science vs. stories – science can be tested and therefore trusted, but Bible stories cannot be tested and therefore cannot be trusted. I do not live a faith-based life; I live a reason-based life, a life that is not founded on fiction but on verifiable science. So Jonah, you'll need to try again.

If that is what you are thinking, thank you for your thoughts.

I will clarify my point using the example of a surgeon performing an operation. Let's say she is performing a critical operation on your heart. She has gone to the best medical school and graduated with honors, she now practices at an excellent hospital, and works with a superb operating room team, and, let's say she also has 20 years of experience in this exact type of surgery. Beyond all this, you have met her, you like her, and what's more: you trust her. She holds the scalpel in her hand and you have faith in her and her team. You have faith that no one has forgotten to sterilize a piece of equipment, no one has miscalculated the level of sedatives that will put you under, no member of the operating team failed to get a full night's rest, or experiences personal problems that might prevent them from performing at their best, no one has incorrectly classified your blood type, or perhaps worst of all (and this has happened) no one at the hospital has mixed up your records with someone else's. As you undergo the operation, you have, my agnostic friend, implicitly made a faith-based decision. You just do not wish to admit it.

Science is very advantageous. We understand science, which is to say, nature's law and rules, because we use reason to understand nature's laws. We place our trust that decisions made with scientific understanding are correct and that declarations, or the testimonies made by scientists, are true – we have faith in scientists, don't we?

Here is another lesson about our faith in scientists. I live not far from Washington, D.C. and not many years ago, a Virginia earthquake shook the Mid-Atlantic from New York to Alabama, with an earthquake powerful enough to put a crack in the Washington Monument. The Washington National Cathedral was also damaged by the earthquake and needed $25 million in repairs. It was the strongest earthquake in Virginia in 117 years.

A nuclear power plant operating 12 miles from the quake's epicenter automatically shut down during the earthquake, as it was designed to do. The power plant appeared to suffer only minor damage. However the earthquake neared the threshold of the nuclear power plant's design specifications – the quake registered at 5.8 and the plant was designed to withstand a 6.2 quake without serious damage.

I found one report on this earthquake especially interesting. Here's an excerpt:

> Plants built a generation ago were designed to withstand an earthquake larger than any known to have occurred in the area. But since then, scientists have been able to better estimate the earthquakes that are possible. And in some cases, those rare quakes could be larger and more frequent than those the plants were designed for.
>
> "If they met a certain level, they didn't look any further," Gregory Hardy, an industry consultant at Simpson, Gumpertz and Hegger in Newport Beach, Calif., said

of some of the industry's earlier assessments. "Forty years ago, when some of these plants were started, the hazard – we had no idea. No one did."[4]

"We had no idea. No one did." Clearly scientists failed to gauge the true level of danger. You see what's going on: scientists can miscalculate on terribly important matters, about issues that can mean life or death, and about things that can mean massive disaster. But still we trust them. My point is that science should be respected, but that we should also maintain a degree of skepticism about scientific conclusions.

An agnostic reader might have another comment:

> Occasional miscalculations aside, I will take science any day over the fabrications of religious belief and silly stories. Science may be inaccurate and even wrong at times, but you can never prove religious beliefs are ever right.

If anyone agrees with the foregoing paragraph, I think they have acknowledged my main point: belief in science has an element of trust, an element of faith. And that faith in science is, as I said earlier, based on trust and faith in scientific testimony, in the testimony of scientists, who can make mistakes in their science and in their testimony. It has even happened that scientists have, rarely, falsified scientific data, reports, or testimony, to advance a viewpoint, whether for commercial or political reasons, or in order to procure government funding for their research.

We base our lives on faith, some of us more than others, but no one has ever made a significant decision without involving a degree faith. We all live faith-based lives. This is not just the *act of faith*; this is *the fact of faith* everyday in every life.

---

[4] The Associated Press, September 2, 2011, Quake risk greater than thought

Christians base their faith on the testimony of the Word of God. The Word of God contains no error.

Christians know the testimony in Acts (4:20 NASB) in which Peter and John are warned by Jewish rulers, elders, and scribes, not to speak or teach in the name of Jesus. Peter and John answered this way, "We cannot stop speaking about what we have seen and heard."

Christians read the beginning of Luke's Gospel where he writes of "original eyewitnesses" who handed down a report of what they saw, and that Luke decided, after investigating everything, to write down an orderly sequence so that Theophilus would have "authentic knowledge" about events that took place. **See Luke 1:1-4**

For Christians, faith is trust in Truth.

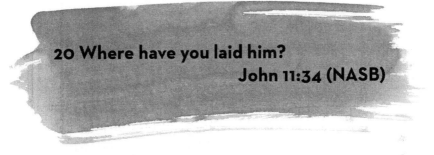

20 Where have you laid him?
John 11:34 (NASB)

Where have you laid him?
John 11:34 (NASB)

Did I not say to you if you believe, you will see the glory of God?
John 11:40 (NASB)

When Jesus asked Mary and Martha these two questions, which I treat as closely related questions, the women were in mourning because their brother Lazarus had just died. I expect many readers are familiar with this story, but even if you are, carefully reread John's 11th chapter and then return here.

In outline, the story is that Mary and Martha send Jesus word about their brother,

> **"Sir, you should know that your friend lies ill."**
> **John 11:3**

To this news, Jesus says:

> **This sickness is not to end in death, but for the glory of God, so that the Son of Man may be glorified by it.**
> **John 11:4 (NASB)**

The Twelve were likely confused by Jesus' words and then even more perplexed by Jesus' decision to stay where he was for two days, before he announced, **"Let us go to Judea again." John 11:7 (NASB)**

Going to Judea was dangerous and the Disciples knew it, because Bethany was only two miles from Jerusalem where Jesus' teachings had attracted determined enemies.

> **The disciples said to Him, "Rabbi, the Jews were just now seeking to stone You, and You are going there again?"**
> **John 11:8 (NASB)**

Jesus is undeterred causing the doomster Thomas to say to the others, **"Let us also go and die with him." John 11:16**

But Lazarus was now dead as Jesus and his men neared Bethany. Jews believed a deceased person's soul lingered near the body for three days, hoping to reenter it, but since Lazarus had now been dead four days, there was no possibility of the departed soul returning to its body, except at the resurrection.[5]

When Jesus is very close to Bethany, Martha and Mary go out to meet Jesus and tell him Lazarus would not have died, if he had been there.

Jesus asks Mary, **"Where have you laid him?"** Arriving at Lazarus' tomb, Jesus tells them to take away the stone covering the tomb's entrance; Mary is concerned about the odor of death after four days, but Jesus says, **"Did I not say to you if you believe, you will see the glory of God?"** John 11:40 (NASB)

Jesus cried out in a loud voice, **"Lazarus, come out!"** (John 11:43) We know the effect of Jesus' words.

If you think about these two questions of Jesus, they are a great contradiction.

"Where have you laid him?"

"Did I not say to you if you believe, you will see the glory of God?"

The first question tells us Jesus had to ask Mary for basic information – where was Lazarus' tomb? Wouldn't the Son of God already know that and have no need to ask where it was? But it seems Jesus must ask, and then goes to the tomb and commands Lazarus to rise from the dead – which was certainly a miracle. Yet, Jesus' two questions to Martha and Mary still present a tremendous contradiction: at one moment Jesus appears to have ordinary, limited human knowledge ("Where have you laid him?"), and at the next moment, Jesus shows God has given him power over humanity's old enemy – death. **"Lazarus, come out!"**

---

[5] Zondervan, NASB Study Bible, New American Study Bible, page 1540

Thus a mysterious contradiction: Jesus of Nazareth seems to have ordinary, limited human knowledge, yet he is also the Son of God.

Jesus of Nazareth is a man, a human, a Jew, a descendant of David. Then again, Jesus of Nazareth is the Son of God and unlike any human. To us it seems a contradiction: Jesus is a human but at the same time the Son of God. To God it is a great harmony.

We see a divine mystery but cannot comprehend it; yet, Jesus gives us insights into this enigma. Consider Jesus' words in John:

> **To deny honour to the Son is to deny it to the Father who sent him.**
>
> **John 5:23**

> **Jesus said to them, "If God were your father, you would love me, for God is the source of my being, and from him I come. I have not come of my accord; he sent me."**
>
> **John 8:42**

> **Jesus said, "In very truth I tell you, before Abraham was born, I am."**
>
> **John 8:58**

> **The Father and I are one.**
>
> **John 10:30**

> **Jesus replied, "I am the way, the truth, and the life; no one comes to the Father except by me."**
>
> **John 14:6**

> **Believe me that I am in the Father and the Father is in Me; otherwise believe because of the works themselves.**
>
> **John 14:11 (NASB)**

Jesus forewarns his fellow Jews that Moses will be their accuser at Judgment. Why? Because they believe that Moses discredits Jesus, while in fact Moses and the prophets validate Jesus. They are expecting praise from Moses, but they will receive his condemnation for their disbelief. The Jewish Bible is the key. Failing to understand Moses and the prophets means a failure to recognize the Messiah. *Jesus was a Jew who came to Jews to explain Jewish Law and to fulfill Jewish prophecy.*

How can you believe when you accept honour from one another, and care nothing for the honour that comes from him who alone is God? Do not imagine that I shall be your accuser at the Father's tribunal. Your accuser is Moses, the very Moses on whom you have set your hope. If you believed him you would believe me, for it was of me that he wrote. But if you do not believe what he wrote, how are you to believe what I say?

John 5:44-47

A grim future lie ahead for disbelieving Pharisees and Jesus tells them why.

Those of the Pharisees who were with Him heard these things and said to Him, "We are not blind too, are we?" Jesus said to them, "If you were blind, you would have no sin; but since you say, 'We see,' your sin remains."

John 9:40-41 (NASB)

Reader note: Questions 21 and 22 both concern John the Baptist, and we will consider them together.

21 What was the spectacle that drew you to the wilderness? A reed swaying in the wind?

Matthew 11:7

Jesus began to speak to the crowds about John: 'What was the spectacle that drew you to the wilderness? A reed swaying in the wind? No? Then what did you go out to see? A man dressed in finery? Fine clothes are to be found in palaces. But why did you go out? To see a prophet? Yes, indeed, and far more than a prophet. He is a man of whom the scripture says,

> Here is my herald, whom I send ahead of you, and he will prepare your way before you.

Truly I tell you: among all who have ever been born, no one has been greater than John the Baptist, and yet the least in the kingdom of Heaven is greater than he.

Matthew 11:7-11

22 How can I describe the people of this generation?

Luke 7:31

> **How can I describe the people of this generation? What are they like? They are like children sitting in the market-place and calling to each other,**
>
> > **We piped for you and you would not dance, We lamented, and you would not mourn.**
>
> **For John the Baptist came, neither eating bread nor drinking wine, and you say, "He is possessed." The Son of Man came, eating and drinking, and they say, "Look at him! A glutton and drinker, a friend of tax-collectors and sinners!" Yet God's wisdom is proved right by all who are its children.**
>
> **Luke 7:31-35**

To test the people's understanding of John the Baptist, Jesus asks them what *they think* about John the Baptist before Jesus reveals what *he knows* about him – and what Jesus knows is that no one born is greater than the Baptist.

> **And if you are willing to accept *it*, John himself is Elijah who was to come.**
>
> **Matthew 11:14 (NASB)**

John the Baptist's clothes were made from course animal hair and his followers frequently fasted, ate insects and honey, which were the food of poor people. His life was different in every respect from ours, we the comfortable Western Christians who are aware that Christians in other parts of the world are being tortured and executed for following the Messiah. We read of an Iranian Christian sentenced to death because he believes Jesus of Nazareth is the Son of God. We read of Christians in the Middle East being brutally executed. Jesus predicted this and warned followers it would happen.

Jesus hears the exasperating attacks on the Baptist's fasting and avoidance of wine – yet these same critics attack Jesus for – are you ready? – for eating and drinking wine! We all know people like this – they are inconsistent; change their line of attack, and make contradictory accusations. They seem unable to remember what they said a few minutes ago. As Ecclesiastes (1:9 NASB) says, "So there is nothing new under the sun." And just as Jesus faced lying critics, so do many followers of the Messiah today.

> **For John the Baptist came, neither eating bread nor drinking wine, and you say, "He is possessed." The Son of Man came, eating and drinking, and they say, "Look at him! A glutton and drinker, a friend of tax-collectors and sinners!"**
>
> **Luke 7:33-34**

Questions 21 and 22 are about recognition: do people recognize the Baptist as a prophet? Do they recognize him as Elijah? And there is an implied question: do they recognize Jesus performs miracles through the power of God?

23 As for you, Capernaum, will you be exalted to heaven? No, you will be brought down to Hades!

Luke 10:15

> **Alas for you, Chorazin! Alas for you, Bethsaida! If the miracles performed in you had taken place in Tyre and Sidon, they would have repented long ago, sitting in sackcloth and ashes. But it will be more bearable for Tyre and Sidon at the**

judgement than for you. As for you, Capernaum, will you be exalted to heaven? No, you will be brought down to Hades!

Luke 10:13-10:15

As these cities reject evidence of miracles – Jesus denounces them for rejecting the work of God accomplished in them. Carefully consider Luke 10:13-15 because it reveals the concept of collective judgment. If the judgment of God can fall upon whole cities, can it fall upon entire nations?

Reader, please note: Questions 24 has two versions in Matthew and Luke, but both of those versions tie into the same question of Sabbath observance, so they indicated below as 24 a and 24 b.

24 a Have you not read what David did when he and his men were hungry?

Matthew 12:3

24 b I put this question to you: is it permitted to do good or to do evil on the sabbath, to save life or to destroy it?

Luke 6:9

When the Pharisees saw this, they said to him, "Look, your disciples are doing what is forbidden on the Sabbath." He answered, "Have you not read

what David did when he and his men were hungry? He went into the house of God and ate the sacred bread, though neither he nor his men had a right to eat it, but only the priests. Or have you not read in the law that on the sabbath the priests serving in the temple break the Sabbath and they are not held to be guilty?"

Matthew 12:2-5

There was a man in the congregation whose right arm was withered; and the scribes and Pharisees were on the watch to see whether Jesus would heal him on the sabbath, so that they could find a charge to bring against him. But he knew what was in their minds and said to the man with the withered arm, "Stand up and come out here." So he stood up and came out. Then Jesus said to them, "I put this question to you: is it permitted to do good or to do evil on the sabbath, to save life or to destroy it?" He looked round at them all, and then he said to the man, "Stretch out your arm." He did so, and his arm was restored. But they totally failed to understand, and began to discuss with one another what they could do to Jesus.

Luke 6:6-11

Sabbath laws were a flashpoint between Jesus and religious authorities. Read this in the Book of Exodus 20:8-11 about the Sabbath law, which, as you know, is one of the Ten Commandments.

Remember to keep the Sabbath day holy. You have six days to labor and do all your work; but the seventh day is a Sabbath of the Lord your God; that day you must not do any work, neither you, nor your son or your daughter, your slave or your slave-girl, your cattle, or

the alien residing among you; for in six days the Lord
made the heavens and the earth, the sea, and all that is
in them, and on the seventh day he rested. Therefore
the Lord blessed the Sabbath day and declared it holy.

It might be easy to view Pharisees as malicious-minded men eager
to find Jesus in violation of the Sabbath, and thus provide a reason to
act against Jesus. In fact, some Pharisees were vicious, but as we read
this Sabbath commandment, which was given to Moses by God, we
understand the Pharisee's devotion to the Sabbath and the Law. And
even though many Pharisees misinterpreted it, we see the Sabbath
law seemed to offer no exceptions.

To understand the seriousness with which Jews understood the
Sabbath, here are two stories, one is ancient and one is modern. First,
the modern story: today, most Jews in Israel are secular, just as there
is a large secular population (Jewish and Gentile) in Europe and the
U.S. At the same time, there are religious neighborhoods in Israel,
particularly in Jerusalem. In these religious areas, the Orthodox
Jews living in them are offended to see cars driven on the Sabbath,
and if they see someone driving a car, the Orthodox Jews, in their
long, black-frocked clothing, have been known to throw stones at the
drivers who are breaking the Sabbath.

Now for an ancient story that shows the seriousness with which Jews
observed the Sabbath. Less then two centuries before Jesus was born,
Israel was oppressed by the Seleucid king Antiochus Epiphanes,
who had conquered Israel, and under threat of violence, Antiochus
made Jews renounce their traditions. But some Jews refused to
obey King Antiochus and hid themselves in the wilderness with
their wives, children, and cattle. King Antiochus Epiphanes' men
heard about these Jews, found them, and ordered them to obey, but
these Jews continue to refuse. So the king's soldiers simply waited
for the Sabbath to attack, knowing these religious Jews would not
profane the Sabbath by fighting – not even to defend themselves.

King Antiochus Epiphanes' men killed one thousand Jews who wouldn't break the Sabbath. The Israelites subsequently concluded that defending themselves on the Sabbath must be allowed.

These stories show the importance of the Sabbath to Jewish life – how could it not be? To the Pharisees, Jesus was breaking the Holiness of the Sabbath, but Jesus' purpose was to actualize the law and fulfill it. And note Jesus used the deeds of King David to prove he understood the Sabbath better than his critics – even though they were experts in the Law. It required a Messiah with God-given wisdom to refocus the Sabbath Law on the larger principles of obedience to God. Pharisees saw that Jesus' redefining of the Sabbath meant his teachings had greater authority than Moses, and greater authority than the Pharisees and than the religious leaders – and those were challenges to their status that they would not accept.

> 25 And if it is Satan who drives out Satan, he is divided against himself; how then can his kingdom stand? If it is by Beelzebul that I drive out devils, by whom do your own people drive them out?
>
> Matthew 12:26-27

If this is your argument, they themselves will refute you. But if it is by the Spirit of God that I drive out the devils, then be sure that the Kingdom of God has already come upon you.

Matthew 12:27-28

Matthew paints a picture of a man who is not only deaf and dumb but also possessed. The benighted man is brought to Jesus who cures him of every ill, yet the Pharisees, rather than praise God for the merciful healing they have learned of, attack Jesus and claim he works through Satan.

"Knowing what was in their minds," Jesus responds with common sense and asks them if Satan destroys Satan, how can his Kingdom stand? And then Jesus asks another question: if he is curing through Satan, who then gives your people the power to drive out Satan? "If this is your argument," Jesus adds, "they themselves will refute you."

As in Luke (7:33), here is another example of inconsistent arguments being used against Jesus and John the Baptist. Jesus' lying adversaries change their lines of attack, reverse their previous positions, and hope no one recalls what they said minutes before. Many times Jesus speaks mysteriously, but not here, here he simply uses common sense, which is enough.

> 26 Or again, how can anyone break into a strong man's house and make off with his goods, unless he has first tied up the strong man?
>
> Matthew 12:29

Or again, how can anyone break into a strong man's house and make off with his goods, unless he has first tied up the strong man? Then he can ransack the house.

Matthew 12:29

Who is this robber in this parable? It's Jesus!

The question causes us to ask ourselves: why does Jesus compare himself to a robber, a thief who breaks into a house to loot it? And who is the strong man Jesus talks about? And what if this strong man has stolen goods in his house? What if the strong man's house has stolen money and he is holding people as hostages? What if the strong man is evil?

And indeed, this is the strong man Jesus tells us about. The strong man is the devil that Jesus ties up and then releases the hostages. How do we know this? Listen to Revelation 20:2, "He seized the dragon, that ancient serpent who is the Devil, or Satan, and chained him up for a thousand years." Revelation is describing the Jewish belief that the devil will be restrained by God's command.

> **27 Viper's brood! How can your words be good when you yourselves are evil?**
>
> **Matthew 12:34**

Get a good tree and its fruit will be good; get a bad tree and its fruit will be bad. You can tell a tree by its fruit. Viper's brood! How can your words be good when you yourselves are evil? It is from the fullness of the heart that the mouth speaks. Good people from their store of good produce good; and evil people from their store of evil produce evil.

Matthew 12:33-35

Jesus uses an analogy that would be readily understood by his fellow Jews, many of whom worked the soil. Jesus reminds them of what they have seen and know: good trees produce good fruit, and bad trees only produce bad fruit. His analogy is a double-edged argument, because his cure of the deaf man validates that his work is good, whereas the Pharisees accusations against Jesus show their words come from their "fullness of heart," which is a "store of evil."

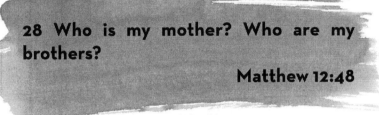

28 Who is my mother? Who are my brothers?

Matthew 12:48

Who is my mother? Who are my brothers?
Matthew 12:48

And looking around him at those who were sitting in the circle around him he said, 'Here are my mother and my brothers. Whoever does the will of my heavenly Father is my brother, and sister, and mother.'
Mark 3:34-35

Clearly, Christian reality is that following the Messiah is to do God's will and in doing His will you become a relative of Jesus; moreover, you become a relative closer and more authentic than natural family bonds.

Note that just before Jesus asked, **"Who is my mother? Who are my brothers?"** he was informed that his family wanted a word with him: "Your mother and your brothers are standing outside; they want to speak to you," (Matthew 12:47), which prompts Jesus to identify his true mother, brother, and sister.

Pointing to his men, Jesus says:

> **Here are my mother and my brothers. Whoever**
> **does the will of my heavenly Father is my brother**
> **and sister and mother.**
>
> **Matthew 12:49-50**

We know this is true and we also know Jesus' words do not permit anyone to neglect natural relations, which obligate due respect and care, especially of the mother and father, if one has the power to do so. No Christian should imagine that these words of Jesus invalidate the Fourth Commandment. Still, Jesus tells us our earthly ties do not equal one's relationship with God – we remember the first commandment: I am the Lord your God who brought you out of Egypt, out of the land of slavery. You must have no other god besides me. (Exodus 20:2-3)

Family relations are important and yet they are subordinate to God. In this way we understand what the Master means when he says, "No one is worthy of me who cares more for father or mother than for me; no one is worthy of me who cares more for son or daughter."

That is from Matthew (10:37) and Jesus states it even more strongly in Luke (14:26):

> If anyone comes to me and does not hate his father
> and mother, wife and children, brothers and sisters,
> and even his own life, he cannot be a disciple of mine.

Many Christians have excellent family relations and they may say, "We encourage each other and live in peace. Why do you talk about disagreement?"

I mention it because the Messiah did. Listen to his words in Luke:

> **Do you suppose I came to establish peace on earth?**
> **No, indeed, I have come to bring dissension. From**

now on, a family of five will be divided, three against two and two against three; father against son and son against father, a mother against daughter, and daughter against mother, mother-in-law against daughter-in-law and daughter-in-law against her mother-in-law.

Luke 12:51-53

I have come to set a man against his father, a daughter against her mother, a daughter-in-law against her mother-in-law; and a man will find his enemies under his own roof.

Matthew 10:35-36

If your family is Christian and absorbs the Bible into their lives, then thanks be to God. But others will be less fortunate and must be prepared for the reality that following the Messiah may make them an enemy to their family. In all cases, God's will be done.

Christians should not imagine it will go well at judgment for one who does not honor their father and mother, nor will it go well for one who values family ties greater than God. The Christian puts first what is first, while fulfilling obligations to respect what should be respected.

29 By the Father's power I have done many good deeds before your eyes; for which of these are you stoning me?

John 10:32

Once again the Jews picked up stones to stone him. At this time Jesus said to them, "By the Father's power I have done many good deeds before your eyes; for which of these are you stoning me?"

"We are not stoning you for any good deed," the Jews replied, "but for blasphemy: you, a man, are claiming to be God." Jesus answered, "Is it not written in your law, 'I said: You are gods'?

John 10:31-34

"It is those to whom God's word came who are called gods – and scripture cannot be set aside. Then why do you charge me with blasphemy for saying, 'I am God's son,' I whom the Father consecrated and sent into the world?"

John 10:35-36

Religious Jews view the name of the God of Israel as sacred and do not think it should be written or even uttered, thus a God-fearing Jew does not presume to write "God" but instead hyphenates the middle letter and writes "G-d", so as not to write the actual word. Thus, as they see God as far above His creation, we see how scandalized Jews were to hear Jesus, who they viewed as only another human, to call himself the Son of God. They thought this was an arrogance deserving of death by stoning.

Jesus knew the scripture well, and told his accusers,

Is it not written in your law, "I said, you are gods"? It is those to whose God's word came who are called gods – and scripture cannot be set aside. Then why do you charge me with blasphemy for saying, "I am God's son," I whom the Father consecrated and sent into the world?

John 10:34-36

The charge of blasphemy meant a potential death sentence for Jesus. We still see today the emotional intensity and the peril of blasphemy charges; I read in the news of a Middle Eastern politician who was assassinated after he had advocated repealing blasphemy laws in his own Muslim country. This politician was assassinated by one of his own guards.

Speaking the truth made Jesus hated by the powers of his time and when Jesus' followers speak the truth it makes them hated by the politically powerful and even by some of our religious elites. Jesus spoke the truth even though doing so brought the death penalty. An end some followers of Jesus meet even now in some countries.

> 30 "What is the kingdom of God like," he continued. "To what shall I compare it?"
> Luke 13:18

Like most urbanites, I knew little about trees until I moved to a more rural environment. Now I can recognize the Red Oaks that grow 90 feet tall. In spring, I see Bluebirds use an oak in my yard as a sentry point to watch over their nest and hatchlings from 70 feet away. In summer, the Red Oak's large, pointed leaves give shade, then in fall they become bright red, as the oak drops hundreds of acorns that deer eat and squirrels store away.

Each Red Oak begins as a small acorn and a mature oak can live for centuries. In fall I gather a few acorns to plant. I reckon if one acorn germinates, it will become a sapling and eventually an adult oak. If it survives its first few years, it likely has more years ahead of it than any human child, grandchild, great grandchild, or even great, great, great grandchild. That tree can outlive any animal on earth.

Back to Jesus describing the Kingdom of God:

> **"What is the kingdom of God like,"** he continued.
> **"To what shall I compare it? It is like a mustard
> seed which a man took and sowed in his garden;
> and it grew to be a tree and the birds came to
> roost among its branches." Again he said, "To what
> shall I compare the kingdom of God? It is like
> yeast which a woman took and mixed with three
> measures of flour till it was all leavened."**
> **Luke 13:18-20**

Many pastors say Jesus uses this parable to teach that the kingdom of God has humble beginnings, but expands over time to a colossal size. I do not disagree, but think about it in a different way. Jesus could have used other trees to describe the kingdom of God: he could have used the majestic cedar, used in construction of the Temple in Jerusalem, or he could have named a wood used to make beautiful furniture, such as Red Oak. After all, he was probably a carpenter who knew about different types of wood. Jesus could have named a wood in his parable that is used in the construction of fishing boats or perhaps a wood used to build warships for Rome, thus indicating the kingdom of God is like a powerful battleship.

Instead he used a mustard seed in his parable, an extremely small seed that grows into a useful, but not a particularly elegant tree. It is more shrub than tree. Of all the seeds on the earth, Jesus used the tiny mustard seed to portray the kingdom of God. When we think about the mustard seed image Jesus used, it is easier to understand the growth, divisions, reunifications, and erratic advance of Christianity, which has not progressed in an easy or evenly paced fashion. And yet the Word of God and the kingdom of God grows, like a mustard seed.

31 Why are you trying to kill me?
John 7:19

"Did not Moses give you the law? Yet not one of you keeps it. Why are you trying to kill me?" The crowd answered, "You are possessed! Who wants to kill you?" Jesus replied, "I did one good deed, and you are all taken aback. But consider: Moses gave you the law of circumcision (not that it originated with Moses, but with the patriarchs) and you circumcise even on the sabbath. Well then, if someone can be circumcised on the sabbath to avoid breaking the law of Moses, why are you indignant with me for making someone's whole body well on the sabbath?"

John 7:19-24

Who is the greater, one who receives the law or the author of the law? The author of course. Who better understands the Law's intention? Jesus better understands the Law's intention because the author of the Law is his Father. The Messiah came to advance understanding of Moses' Law.

When the crowds hear Jesus ask, **"Why are you trying to kill me?"** they believe Jesus is suffering from what psychologists today call a persecutory delusion – a groundless fear of plots directed towards him. The crowds ask Jesus, "Who wants to kill you?" but Jesus knew what his enemies were planning. Jesus did not suffer from psychological delusion – Jesus understood that he threatened a world of lies.

32 You of little faith, why did you doubt? Matthew 14:31 (NASB)

Immediately Jesus stretched out His hand and took hold of him, and said to him, "You of little faith, why did you doubt?"

Matthew 14:31 (NASB)

This is what we know: Jesus had finished teaching for the day and he had miraculously fed 5,000 men with a few fish and loaves of bread, not counting the wives and children who had also eaten of the fish and loaves. Then, as the day was closing, Jesus sent his men across the Sea of Galilee as he stayed behind and prayed. That night, between 3-6 am, when his men had already traveled some distance from shore, they encountered strong headwinds making sailing hard, and then they looked across the waves and they saw Jesus, who seemed to be walking on water. They were terrified and yelled, "It is a ghost!" (Matthew 14:26 NASB) Jesus called out and said he was no ghost.

Peter spoke up, "Lord, if it is You, command me to come to You on the water." And He said, "Come!" And Peter got out of the boat, and walked on the water and came toward Jesus. But seeing the wind, he became frightened, and began to sink, he cried out, "Lord, save me!" Immediately Jesus stretched out His hand and took hold of him, and said to him, **"You of little faith, why did you doubt?"** (Matthew 14:28-31)

Let's make some common-sense assumptions: Peter was a skilled fisherman who knew the Sea of Galilee and had learned to read the weather. Peter was likely to have been a good swimmer. He had sailed all the 64 square miles of the Sea of Galilee, and he knew its shoreline like the back of his hand. He had cast his fishing nets into its 13-mile length and eight-mile width, and he knew what time of day he was most likely to catch fish and what prices they could bring at the market.

Peter was an expert fisherman who did not fear water and he was certain of this – no one walks on water. Yet that was what Peter was doing – walking on water toward Jesus. The Bible says, "But when he saw the strength of the gale" Peter became afraid and started to sink. (Matthew 14:30)

Peter *did* walk on the water *until* when he stopped to think that *he couldn't*. Peter became of two minds – he first believed and then he didn't believe. Peter saw Jesus on the water – in conflict with Peter's knowledge that no one could walk on water, and then Peter also walked on water until he became afraid. The impossible became possible until Peter realized it was impossible.

It is impossible to walk on water. Until someone walks on water.

It is impossible to return from the dead. Until someone returns from the dead.

> 33 And He answered and said to them, "Why do you yourselves transgress the commandment of God for the sake of your tradition?"
>
> Matthew 15:3 (NASB)

Then some Pharisees and scribes came to Jesus from Jerusalem and said, "Why do your disciples break the tradition of the elders? For they do not wash their hands when they eat bread." And He answered and said to them, "Why do you yourselves

transgress the commandment of God for the sake of your tradition?"

Matthew 15:1-3 (NASB)

Jesus' question puts the Pharisees in conflict with the prophets, for the prophets had condemned man-made traditions. Human traditions undermined the Law of Moses by subordinating them to human wants. The Pharisees were proud of keeping the Law, but they kept it in name as they rejected the heart of the law, and Jesus said to them, "You have made God's law null and void out of your regard for your tradition," and he quoted the Prophet Isaiah:

> **"How right Isaiah was when he prophesied about you: 'This people pays me lip-service, but their heart is far from me; they worship me in vain, for they teach as doctrines the commandments of men.'"**
>
>
>
> **Matthew 15:7-9**
>
>

Humans had become skilled at manipulating God's Law for their own benefit. They had been doing this for many years. Listen to the Prophet Jeremiah who lived 600 years before Jesus:

> **"How can you say, 'We are wise,**
> **And the law of the Lord is with us'?**
> **But behold, the lying pen of the scribes**
> **Has made *it* into a lie."**
>
>
>
> **Jeremiah 8:8 (NASB)**
>
>

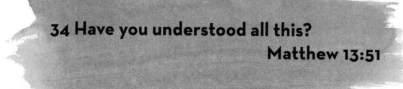

34 Have you understood all this?

Matthew 13:51

That is how it will be at the end of time. The angels will go out, and they will separate the wicked from the good, and throw them into the blazing furnace, where there will be wailing and grinding of teeth. Have you understood all this?

Matthew 13:49-51

Jesus was a teacher and teaching is challenging. Jesus repeatedly asked those he taught: Do you understand what I am saying? Can you understand the truth of this parable?

Jesus liked to use parables as he likely thought using pictures of things that people already knew helps them learn faster. At the same time, Jesus of Nazareth knew the heart of his teachings would be hidden from many, and he knew some people would distort his teachings, sometimes unintentionally, at other times deliberately.

I had the happy experience of working for an amiable man who was smart, highly educated, and quick with one-liners. He was of rounded build and he would have made a good department store Santa Claus because his amiable personality would have endeared him to children. He had spent years teaching at a university and liked to say: "Teaching does not necessarily result in learning."

Everyone in the office liked him. If he'd been an Apostle, I think he would have been thoughtful and good-natured. I could imagine him listening to Jesus teach and when Jesus asked, "Do you understand all these things?" I imagine my former boss saying, "I'm not sure the people understand and I'm not sure I do either," adding, "but teaching does not necessarily result in learning."

Understanding what Jesus of Nazareth taught is why we were born. His question, "Have you understood all this?" is the critical question. After saying that, some might fear they do not have enough education, or Bible study, or theology courses. But no one should worry about that, because the highly educated are in fact disadvantaged in understanding what Jesus of Nazareth taught, as we remember Jesus' words in Luke:

> **At that moment Jesus exulted in the Holy Spirit and said, "I thank you, Father, Lord of heaven and earth, for hiding these things from the learned and wise, and revealing them to the simple. Yes, Father, such was your choice."**
>
> **Luke 10:21**

Jesus did not choose his close circle from educated Pharisees or scribes, but rather he chose fishermen who worked outdoors, and who, if they had any education, it was unlikely to have been very much.

> **35 Jesus said, "Are you still lacking in understanding also?"**
>
> **Matthew 15:16 (NASB)**

> **Peter said to Him, "Explain the parable to us." Jesus said, "Are you still lacking in understanding also? Do you not understand that everything that goes into the mouth passes into the stomach, and is eliminated? But the things that proceed out of the mouth come from the heart, and those defile the man. For out of the heart come evil thoughts, murders, adulteries, fornications, thefts, false witness, slanders. These are the things which defile the man: but to eat with unwashed hands does not defile the man."**
>
> **Matthew 15:15-20 (NASB)**

Jesus is a devoted teacher who is at times discouraged by his slow-witted students. "Are you still lacking in understanding …?" Jesus asks his men when they seem confused by his teaching on ritual hand-washing.

The first thing to note is that Jesus was not addressing the use of soap. The Pharisees didn't have soap. Even the notion of soap as a disinfectant was unknown. Bacteria had not yet been discovered and the microscopic world of germs wouldn't be detected for centuries. Thus the Pharisees were not washing their hands for sanitary reasons, but for symbolic purity, and to a degree to remove dirt. Think of John the Baptist, who, when he baptized people in running water was washing away dirt, to our human eye; but also washing away sin, to the spiritual eye.

Jesus wanted the Pharisees to change their perspective: their tradition of dipping hands in water did not affect their spiritual cleanliness. Jesus listed seven things in the heart, or in today's language, the consciousness, that can pollute a person spiritually: **"evil thoughts, murders, adulteries, fornications, thefts, false witness, slanders."**

Pharisees saw that Jesus of Nazareth was criticizing something fundamental to Judaism – their teachings about which foods Moses allowed and which he had forbidden, and those were serious issues.

Contamination originates in the mind. We daily hear talk about pollution and ecology, about the climate and recycling and sustainability, and while these are important, the issues of spiritual contamination and pollution are of much greater importance. The Christian understands this.

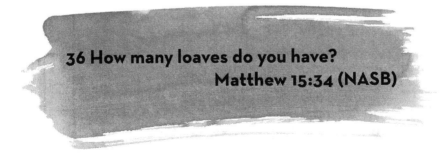

36 How many loaves do you have?
Matthew 15:34 (NASB)

How many loaves do you have?
Matthew 15:34 (NASB)
(also see Matthew 14:13-21)

How many loaves do you have? Go look!
Mark 6:38 (NASB)

How many loaves do you have?
Mark 8:5 (NASB)

Therefore Jesus, lifting up His eyes and seeing that a large crowd was coming to Him, said to Philip, "Where are we to buy bread, so that these may eat?" This He was saying to test him, for He Himself knew what He was intending to do.
John 6:5-6 (NASB)

A day is ending during which Jesus had healed the sick and taught about the Kingdom of Heaven. Now the people are hungry and the apostles rightly worry that if the crowds try to walk to reach a surrounding village to buy food, they might faint on the way.

To address the food shortage, Jesus blesses what is on hand, only a few loaves of bread and a couple of fish, and from this blessed food thousands eat, with baskets full of food left over. All four Gospels report this miracle, but I find John's account the most interesting because it reveals Jesus' thinking and tells us a little more:

It seems Jesus enjoys testing his disciples and friends. Perhaps he wants to see if their faith in God's power is growing. Even though "Jesus himself knew what he meant to do" he still probes Philip's thinking by asking, **"Where are we to buy bread, so that these may eat?"** Jesus seems interested to know if Philip can anticipate how God will work through faith in this situation.

> **37 Knowing what they were discussing, Jesus said, "Why are you talking about having no bread? Where is your faith? Do you still not understand?"**
>
> **Matthew 16:8-9**

In crossing to the other side the disciples had forgotten to take any bread. So when Jesus said to them, "Take care; be on your guard against the leaven of the Pharisees and Sadducees," they began to say to one another, "We have brought no bread!" Knowing what they were discussing, Jesus said, "Why are you talking about having no bread? Where is your faith? Do you still not understand? Have you forgotten the five loaves for the five thousand, and how many basketfuls you picked up? Or the seven loaves for the four thousand, and how many baskets you picked up? How can you fail to see that I was not talking about bread? Be on your guard, I said, against the leaven of the Pharisees and Sadducees." Then they understood: they were to be on their guard, not against bakers' leaven, but against the teachings of the Pharisees and Sadducees.

> Matthew 16:5-12
> (Also, Mark 8:14-21)

The Disciples take Jesus' words literally. And Jesus appears irritated that his men understand him literally, instead of metaphorically and he asks, **"How can you fail to see I was not talking about bread?"**

Jesus confused people – and his words continue to confuse many people today, even some Christians. You are less likely to be one of the confused if you remember Jesus liked to use metaphors. Here are six of his well-known metaphors:

I am the bread of life.	**John 6:35**
I am the light of the world.	**John 8:12**
I am the good shepherd.	**John 10:14**
You are salt to the world.	**Matthew 5:13**
You are the light of the world.	**Matthew 5:14 (NASB)**
I am the true vine, and my Father is the vinedresser.	**John 15:1 (NASB)**

Metaphors communicate a *quality* or *impression*, and all of these metaphors reveal an impression to our minds that Jesus is *bread*, he is the *good shepherd*, and that he is the *true vine*. Thus, in all of these metaphors he tells us that he *shares a quality* with a good shepherd, shares a *quality* with a vine, and shares a *quality* with bread.

Now back to the question Jesus asked his men:

> **"We have brought no bread!" Knowing what they were discussing, Jesus said, "Why are you talking about having no bread? Where is your faith? Do you still not understand?"**
>
> **Matthew 16:7-9**

The Twelve couldn't grasp Jesus' metaphor about the leaven – the characteristic of leaven being that a small amount of leaven changes a large amount of dough. Just so, Jesus told his men through his metaphor that they needed to protect their minds "against the leaven of the Pharisees" (Mark 8:15). Jesus was saying even a small amount of the Pharisees' and Sadducees interpretations can warp what Jesus is saying.

As a Jew speaking to Jews, Jesus' warning about the Pharisees' leaven would have made another connection to his Jewish audience. Here's why: Moses instructed Jews to rid their homes of leaven when preparing to celebrate Passover–Pesach, the Jewish holiday celebrating liberation from Egyptian slavery. During the preparation for Passover-Pesach, any leavened bread was forbidden in the home, because *unleavened* bread was to remind Jews of their Exodus, when they needed to quickly leave Egypt without waiting for their bread to rise – because their liberation was at hand.

This is also true today in religiously observant Jewish homes in Israel and other Jewish communities around the world, where Jewish homes carefully remove any leaven or leavened products before Passover. For religious Jews, even the smallest breadcrumb from their kitchens and homes must be cleaned out.

Now that we understand more clearly about Jesus' example of leaven, let's return to his warning to, "Take care; be on your guard against the leaven of the Pharisees and Sadducees." We can assume the Pharisees, being teachers of the Law, would have "warned" Jewish people to prepare for Passover and remove any leavened bread from their homes. Jesus may have taken that warning from the Pharisees and used it to say: Look! The Pharisees warn you to guard against any leaven in your house during Passover, but I warn you to be on guard against *their* leaven, the *leaven* of the Pharisees (their teachings and hypocrisy) and do not let *their leaven* pollute your thinking.

38 Who do people say that the Son of Man is?

Matthew 16:13

79

When he came to the territory of Caesarea Philippi, Jesus asked his disciples, "Who do people say that the Son of Man is?" They answered, "Some say John the Baptist, others Elijah, others Jeremiah, or one of the prophets." "And you," he asked, "who do you say I am?" Simon Peter answered, "You are the Messiah, the Son of the living God."

Then Jesus said: "Simon son of Jonah, you are favoured indeed! You did not learn that from any human being; it was revealed to you by my heavenly Father.

Matthew 16:13-17

Jesus of Nazareth lived in troubled times. In Israel's villages, towns, and cities, Jews speculated about a Messiah – the one anointed by God – someone they believed would be heroic, like King David. They expected the coming Messiah to end their bitter disagreements amongst themselves and to free them from Rome, just like King David had defeated Israel's enemies and united their nation.

King David is one of history's greatest figures. God chose David the shepherd to become the king of Israel, and chose David's progeny to rule Israel. Jews naturally thought that a Messiah, a new King of the Jews, would be a descendant of David, and that he would have, like King David, military skills, physical strength, and be popular with the people.

Jesus of Nazareth lived at a time of intense Messianic expectations, and when Jesus spoke his fellow Jews heard him within the context of those hopes. So who did Jews at think Jesus was? A wandering rabbi? A prophet? And when he cured the sick and possessed, what did they think about that? Did they see a holy man working through God's power or a magician working through suspect powers?

Jesus asks what people were saying about him, and his men respond, **"Some say John the Baptist, others Elijah, others Jeremiah, or one of the prophets."** Jesus listened, knowing his true identity was hidden from human insight. So he questions those he had taught, those who had seen the miracles, to see if even one knew his true identity.

> **"And you, who do you say I am?"**

> **Simon Peter answered: "You are the Messiah, the Son of the Living God."**

> **Then Jesus said: "Simon son of Jonah, you are favoured indeed! You did not learn that from any human being; it was revealed to you by my heavenly Father."**

Logical analysis would not have given Peter the answer to Jesus' question; God's wisdom gave Peter the answer, and that gift of insight to Peter showed his favor above the eleven others. Jesus put his men under **"strict orders"** not to divulge his identity, and then told them he would die because his words offended the priests, scribes, and elders, but that he would rise from the dead on the third day.

Now they know, Jesus' teachings will meet increasing hatred from his enemies, who will plan to put an end to Jesus and his teachings. His enemies want a final solution to the influence of Jesus.

Peter strongly protests when Jesus tells him the Messiah will be tortured and executed.

> **"At this Peter took hold of him and began to rebuke him: 'Heaven forbid!' he said, 'No, Lord, this shall never happen to you.'"**
>
> **Matthew 16:22**

Jesus immediately reproves Peter: **"Out of my sight, Satan; you are a stumbling block to me. You think as men think, not as God thinks."**

Matthew 16:23

Jesus' words to Peter are a momentous rebuke. Just moments before, Peter was called "favoured indeed" for receiving the divine wisdom to understand Jesus' Messianic identity. Now, just seconds later, Jesus does not call Peter the Rock, but instead says to him, **"Out of my sight, Satan; you are a stumbling block to me. You think as men think, not as God thinks."**

Naturally, Peter does not want his friend to be rejected and die, but Peter's thoughts are no longer divinely inspired. Peter now thinks like an ordinary man, without the inspiration of the Holy Spirit. In fact, Peter was now being inspired by something very different and unholy.

As with Peter, so with us, everyone needs to be cautious that Jesus' rebuke to Peter does not apply to themselves and to their thinking. For just like Peter, at one moment a Christian may be speaking through God's inspiration, and in the next, they may think like an ordinary man or woman, and if one is careless, they may even be promoting the plans of God's adversary. It may be that some Christians, perhaps someone like Saint Francis of Assisi, achieve such a degree of holiness that their hearts and minds are merged with the divine will. That is hard to know, but I do know that for us less advanced Christians, we who are not like the saints we read about, we should be on guard.

39 Do you also want to leave?

John 6:67

> **From that moment many of his disciples drew back**
> **and no longer went about with him. So Jesus asked**
> **the Twelve, "Do you also want to leave?" Simon**
> **Peter answered him, "Lord, to whom shall we go?**
> **Your words are words of eternal life. We believe**
> **and know that you are God's Holy One."**
>
> **John 6:66-69**

We do not know how many disciples left Jesus at this point because John doesn't tell us if it was five or 50 who had decided they'd heard enough. Neither do we know if they decided to leave by individual decision or by vote, nor if those who left had been sent by the Pharisees to infiltrate Jesus' followers to incite disagreement. We do not know.

We do know that before these men left, they had heard Jesus say he was the living bread and anyone who ate this bread would live forever. Jesus' language began a "fierce dispute" among Jews, at which point Jesus further shocked them by saying:

> **My flesh is real food; my blood is real drink.**
>
> **John 6:55**

When Jesus said this, he was probably well known as a rabbi, miracle worker, and holy man. So when he visited the Capernaum synagogue, Jews there would have welcomed him and been interested to hear him. But what they heard was repulsive. They did not expect this religious man to say cannibalism would bring eternal life.

Jesus' words offended Jewish listeners even more than we imagine. To hear Jesus prescribe cannibalism would have been revolting, but to hear him talk about drinking blood would have intensified that disgust, because in the early books of the Bible, the Pentateuch, it is written: God blessed Noah after the flood and told him all the creatures are food for you, **"Only you shall not each flesh with its life,** *that is***, its blood." Genesis 9:4 (NASB)**

To Jewish ears, Jesus had offended the law, but even worse than that, Jesus called his blood real drink and those who drank it would have eternal life, thus directly offending Moses, who said: **"It is a perpetual statute throughout your generations in all your dwellings: you shall not eat any fat or any blood." (Leviticus 3:17 NASB)**

These prohibitions against blood are part of Jewish kosher laws concerning the slaughter of animals and they were meant to reduce the suffering of the animal being sacrificed and ensure all of its blood was drained. With this crystal clear prohibition against consuming blood in the Old Testament, we understand the reaction of the Jews who heard Jesus' words: **"This is more than we can stand! How can anyone listen to such talk?" John 6:60**

> **Jesus was aware that his disciples were grumbling about it and asked them, "Does this shock you? Then what if you see the Son of Man ascending to where he was before? It is the spirit that gives life; the flesh can achieve nothing; the words I have spoken to you are both spirit and life."**
>
> **John 6:61-63**

The *words* Jesus speaks are spirit and life. His *words* are the flesh and blood. Again, people are confused by the correspondence of the literal and the metaphorical.

Still, Matthew, John, Andrew and the other nine Disciples are shocked at Jesus' words, but Jesus doesn't soften his message, he instead stretches their minds to understand that he came from heaven and he will return there and they will see his ascension.

40 and no one who lives and has faith in me shall ever die. Do you believe this?

John 11:26

> Jesus said, "I am the resurrection and the life. Whoever has faith in me shall live, even though he dies; and no one who lives and has faith in me shall ever die. Do you believe this?" "I do, Lord," she answered; "I believe that you are the Messiah, the Son of God who has come into the world."
>
> **John 11:25-27**

Jesus completely identifies himself with eternal life, faith, and the resurrection, **"Do you believe this?"** he asks Martha. Martha's answer tells us Jesus is now recognized as the Messiah, not only by Peter and the disciples, but also within a circle of friends.

With Jesus' words shocking Jews and the disciples, how did *any* of them accept him as the Messiah?

John's sixth chapter explains how:

> And He was saying, "For this reason I have said to you, that no one can come to Me unless it has been granted him from the Father."
>
> **John 6:65 (NASB)**

Understanding Jesus is the Messiah is a God-given gift of wisdom.

We return to the questions contained in John 6:

> **So Jesus asked the Twelve, "Do you also want to leave?" Simon Peter answered him, "Lord, to whom shall we go? Your words are words of eternal life. We believe and know that you are God's Holy One."**
>
> **John 6:67-69**

We sense pessimism when Jesus asks, **"Do you also want to leave?"** Jesus reveals more, yet loses friends when he does. Some of his followers did not understand what he said, became offended and left. Now Jesus wonders if even his closest friends will leave. Moments earlier the Messiah said his flesh must be eaten and his blood drunk, but now he sounds like an ordinary human, who thinks his best friends might turn away.

Notice Peter did not say, "We believe and *understand you*," but "We believe and know that you are God's Holy One." Peter said, "Believe and know," not believe and understand. I think Peter said that because Jesus taught much that is difficult to understand. For now, Peter and the disciples remain loyal to Jesus, but a harder test is ahead for the disciples.

When Peter spoke, did he speak for the other eleven disciples or only for the ten disciples? Because Jesus knew one disciple was an enemy. **"Have I not chosen the twelve of you? Yet one of you is a devil."** **He meant Judas son of Simon Iscariot.**

John 6:70

> **41 Anyone who has seen me has seen the Father. Then how can you say, "Show us the Father"?**
>
> **John 14:9**

Have I been all this time with you, Philip, and still you do not know me? Anyone who has seen me has seen the Father. Then how can you say, "Show us the Father"? Do you not believe that I am in the Father and the Father in me?

John 14:9-10

Jesus responds to Philip's request with a question, "How can you say, 'Show us the Father?'" Jesus seems disappointed at Philip's question and his failure to understand. Jesus seems to think that by now Philip should understand that the Messiah's relationship to God is so profound they live in each other – and says to Philip that Jesus' words are not his own but that **"I am not myself the source of the words I speak to you: it is the Father who dwells in me doing his own work."**

John 14:10

This claim shocked Jews 2,000 years ago and remains a leading reason why Jews and many Gentiles cannot accept Jesus is the Messiah, as they view the idea of God dwelling in a human, even a holy one like Jesus, to be incomprehensible and sacrilegious. For followers of the Messiah, Jesus is indeed the Son of God. Every Christian believes it and earlier Christians were put to death for believing it, and today, in some places and nations, Christians are executed for believing Jesus is the Son of God.

This question perplexed Jesus' parents (see Q1) and continues to confuse the world today: That the God of the Universe is the Father of Jesus. Remember the first question Jesus asked his parents when they found him in the Temple.

His parents were astonished to see him there, and his mother said to him, "My son, why have you treated us like this? Your father and I have been anxiously searching for you." "Why did you search for me?" he said,

"Did you not know that I was bound to be in my Father's house?" But they did not understand what he meant.

Luke 2:48-50

Young Jesus spoke the truth to his parents and he would much later say as an adult:

Believe when I say that I am in the Father and the Father in me; or else accept the evidence of the deeds themselves.

John 14:11

42 What will anyone gain by winning the whole world at the cost of his life? Or what can he give to buy his life back?

Matthew 16:25-26

Jesus then said to his disciples, "Anyone who wishes to be a follower of mine must renounce self; he must take up his cross and follow me. Whoever wants to save his life will lose it, but whoever loses his life for my sake will find it. What will anyone gain by winning the whole world at the cost of his life? Or what can he give to buy his life back?"

Matthew 16:24-26

Jesus taught anyone who would follow him a simple but extremely demanding lesson: deny one's self, pick up your cross and follow.

You may be thinking that Jesus' message of self-denial and carrying a cross does not sound like the messages you hear from some of today's Christian leaders. We hear popular leaders of large Christian congregations preaching that Jesus brings good health, blessings, and prosperity.

I am not going to argue with these Christian leaders because good health, blessings, and prosperity do come to many followers of Jesus of Nazareth. However, I think Christians need a broader perspective of Jesus' teachings, and contemplating his questions is a good way to see the bigger perspective.

A person joining the United States Army takes an oath to support and defend the Constitution of the United States against all enemies, foreign and domestic, and to "bear true faith and allegiance to the same." The oath includes obeying orders of the President of the United States, and of those officers appointed in the chain of command above the individual. The oath ends, "so help me God."

Every soldier, sailor, airmen, and marine is trained to use weapons, even though not all service members serve in combat roles. Some are mechanics, some medics, some train new recruits, others are translators, and many work in administrative supporting roles, but each member of the military is capable of combat. Each soldier has left their former life and understands suffering and even death is possible, and in some places and at some times, it may even be a likely prospect.

So it is with Christians. Every Christian takes an oath to God through the Messiah to live in allegiance to the Truth. Each Christian is a soldier against the adversary, but each Christian serves in a different capacity. They have left their former life in order to follow the Messiah, whatever that may mean for them personally. Jesus teaches his followers that suffering is a definite possibility, and at some times and places, almost a certainty.

> **43 For what is a man profited if he gains the whole world, and loses or forfeits himself?**
>
> **Luke 9:25 (NASB)**

For whoever wishes to save his life will lose it; but whoever loses his life for My sake will find it.
Matthew 16:25 (NASB)

For what is a man profited if he gains the whole world, and loses or forfeits himself?
Luke 9:25 (NASB)

This question parallels Q 42, but Jesus' question about "winning the whole world at the cost of destroying himself" can be understood in several ways.

If you want to know the value of a house, you can check comparables in the neighborhood. If you want to know the value of a car, you can check it on the Internet, but what about the value of a soul? Jesus' question tells us the soul is priceless.

Gold experts estimate only 165,000 tons of gold have been mined in all of human history; but even if you owned every ounce of it you would not be able to avoid judgment.

The world's wealthiest billionaires have established "The Giving Pledge" society, a group whose members pledge to give away half of their wealth. I think they should have named it the Zacchaeus Club, after the wealthy man Zacchaeus who gave away half his riches. Luke (19:8) tells the story of Jesus going to Zacchaeus' home for dinner, the host was so profoundly affected by Jesus' words, it caused Zacchaeus to pledge: "Here and now, sir, I give half my possessions to charity; and if I have defrauded anyone, I will repay him four times over." Jesus said to Zacchaeus:

> "Today salvation has come to this house, because
> he, too, is a son of Abraham. For the Son of Man has
> come to seek and to save which was lost."
>
> Luke 19:9-10 (NASB)

The Giving Pledge club's generosity is impressive, yet we remember another rich man, to whom Jesus said: "Sell everything you have and give it to the poor, and you will have treasure in heaven, then come and follow me." When the rich man declined the invitation, Jesus said, **"How hard it is for those who are wealthy to enter the kingdom of God! For it is easier for a camel to go through the eye of a needle than for a rich man to enter the kingdom of God."**

> **Luke 18:24-25 (NASB)**

Jesus also said:

> **Beware, and be on your guard against every form
> of greed; for not *even* when one has an abundance
> does his life consist of his possessions.**
>
> **Luke 12:15 (NASB)**

And again, Jesus said:

> **So then, none of you can be My disciple who does
> not give up all his own possessions.**
>
> **Luke 14:33 (NASB)**

When "The Giving Pledge" members donate half their wealth, will it mean they stopped half way to heaven? Only God knows.

44 Or what king will march to battle against another king, without first sitting down to consider whether with ten thousand men he can face an enemy coming to meet him with twenty thousand?

Luke 14:31

Or what king will march to battle against another king, without first sitting down to consider whether with ten thousand men he can face an enemy coming to meet him with twenty thousand? If he cannot, then, long before the enemy approaches, he sends envoys and asks for terms.

Luke 14:31-32

In 55 B.C., Julius Caesar sailed two legions and 80 ships to Britain's southern coast in fair weather, planning to conquer Britain. But the native Britons fought Caesar's legionnaires from a superior position – the commanding heights above the beach and thus prevented Caesar's legions from completing their assault, even though the Romans were 20,000 men strong. Britain's weather also turned against the Romans and they were unable to conquer Britain until 90 years later. Julius Caesar won many battles, but he failed to calculate the cost in this one.

Christians should calculate the cost of discipleship. **"Or what king will march to battle against another king, without first sitting down to consider whether with ten thousand men he can face an enemy coming to meet him with twenty thousand?"**

Jesus taught people to reckon the cost of what lies ahead and used an example of constructing a tower.

"Would any of you think of building a tower without first sitting down and calculating the cost, to see whether he could afford to finish it?"

Luke 14:28

Paul, too, used the example of building in Corinthians:

According to the grace of God which was given to me, like a wise master builder, I laid a foundation, and another is building on it. But each man must be careful how he builds on it. For no man can lay a foundation other than the one which is laid, which is Jesus Christ.

1 Corinthians 3:10-11 (NASB)

45 And Jesus answered and said, "You unbelieving and perverse generation, how long shall I be with you and put up with you? Bring your son here."

Luke 9:41 (NASB)

How long has this been happening to him?

Mark 9:21 (NASB)

And Jesus answered and said, "You unbelieving and perverted generation, how long shall I be with you and put up with you? Bring your son here."

Luke 9:41 (NASB)
(also Mark 9:19)

Jesus and Peter, John, and James were returning from a trip and find the other disciples surrounded by a crowd and arguing with scribes. When the crowd notices Jesus they run to him, and Jesus asks them what the disturbance is about. A pitiful man speaks up and says his only son is possessed, and that he had asked Jesus' disciples to cure him, but they could not.

"And a man from the crowd shouted, saying, 'Teacher, I beg You to look at my son, for he is my only *boy.* (Luke 9:38 NASB), "But if you can do anything, take pity on us and help us!" And Jesus said to him, "'If You can?' All things are possible to him who believes." Immediately the boy's father cried out and said, "I do believe; help my unbelief." (Mark 9:23-24 NASB)

Note Jesus' question: **"How long has this been happening to him?"** in Mark 9:21 (NASB). Why would Jesus ask that? Why did it matter? Can we infer that if the afflicted man had only been like that for "a few days or a few weeks" Jesus would have then known his disciples could not exorcise a less established evil spirit?

But since the father told Jesus his son had been afflicted from "childhood," Jesus may have concluded his disciples were dealing with a powerfully entrenched evil spirit, thus when his men later asked Jesus why they had failed, Jesus said, "This kind cannot come out by anything but prayer." (Mark 9:29 NASB)

Jesus' question tells his men and us that some demons are stronger than others, and that spiritual training and discipline is necessary to prepare for that kind of difficult spiritual work. The stronger the adversary then the greater the faith in God and the longer the spiritual preparation necessary to defeat it.

The second idea within Jesus' question relates to our 21st century perspective. We might think those backward people thought the boy was possessed, while we moderns may view the boy as epileptic – because he foams at the mouth, grinds his teeth, goes rigid and appears to throw himself into fire and water. So we might wonder, did Jesus cure a neurological disorder such as epilepsy, or did he remove an evil spirit from the boy? This question might be an interesting point of discussion for a Bible study.

> **46 Why do you not understand what I am saying? It is because my teaching is beyond your grasp.**
>
> **John 8:43**

They said, "We are not illegitimate; God is our father, and God alone." Jesus said to them, "If God were your Father, you would love me, for God is the source of my being, and from him I come. I have not come of my own accord; he sent me. Why do you not understand what I am saying? It is because my teaching is beyond your grasp. Your father is the devil and you choose to carry your father's desires. He was a murderer from the beginning, and is not rooted in the truth; there is no truth in him. When he tells a lie he is speaking his own language, for he is a liar and the father of lies. But because I speak the truth, you do not believe me. Which of you can convict me of sin? If what I say is true, why do you not believe me?"

John 8:41-46

They are priests, Pharisees, and Sadducees and they are respected experts who enjoy good relations with their government, which is supported by Caesar. Some of these Pharisees and Sadducees might be considered to function as the lobbyists of their day and Jesus enrages them. They don't like Jesus' popularity. They don't like the miracles, which seem to move with Jesus; even Jesus' birth has mystery surrounding it. Jesus denounces them and so they think, "Who is this Jesus of Nazareth to say the devil is our father? We've heard the rumors from Nazareth that Jesus is the one without a father!" So they reply: **"We are not illegitimate; God is our father, and God alone."**

Jesus responds: **"Why do you not understand what I am saying? It is because my teaching is beyond your grasp."** As his opponents wonder about Jesus' religious training, Jesus says, **"In very truth I tell you, if anyone obeys my teaching he will never see death."** (John 8:51) Jesus' enemies think, "Are you greater than our father Abraham? He is dead and the prophets too are dead. Who do you claim to be?"

(John 8:53)

Perhaps the Pharisees started to think, "This Jesus tells illiterate villagers that whoever believes in him will never die. Well, maybe we should let him taste death. After all, if his followers will never die, then Jesus must think he himself will never die, right?"

This is an argument between Jews – between Jesus and the Pharisees – and argument about their fathers and forefathers. "Your father is the devil and you choose to carry out your father's desires," Jesus says to them.

They respond: **"We are not illegitimate; God is our father, and God alone."**

John 8:41

Wait! *What did they say?* They said God is *their* father and thus *they must* be *sons of God*! Yet, they turn around and *attack Jesus for claiming he is the Son of God!* Hypocrites and liars – one minute they claim that they are God's sons, and the next minute they say Jesus of Nazareth should die for claiming the same thing.

God's judgment fell on Jerusalem for its treatment of Jesus. Forty years after Jesus was crucified in Jerusalem, to the very day, on Passover, the Roman Commander Titus entered the gates of Jerusalem and that city suffered death on a colossal scale. The famous Jewish historian Flavius Josephus was there to witness it and he said the dead totaled more than 1,100,000.

On the night they seized Jesus, a traitor guided them to the man, who was then brought before a night council of elders, chief priests, and scribes. That council asked Jesus of Nazareth the all-important question:

> **And they all said, "Are You the Son of God, then?"**
> **And He said to them, "Yes, I am." Then they said,**
> **"What further need do we have of testimony? For**
> **we have heard it ourselves from His own mouth."**
> **Luke 22:70-71 (NASB)**

They put Jesus the prisoner before Pontius Pilate, but the Roman governor saw their accusations against Jesus as an issue of relevance only to Jews, so Pilate is indifferent and says, "Take Him yourselves, and judge Him according to your law." (John 18:31 NASB)

But Jesus' accusers need Pilate's approval for two reasons. First, they want Rome's involvement, Rome's entanglement, because it not only extends blame for Jesus' death, but Rome's involvement would further discredit Jesus – he would then face execution by Gentiles, who were viewed as unclean foreigners by Jews. They want shared blame because Jesus is popular and the leading Pharisees and priests do not want to be seen as the sole authority responsible for his execution. Although they reject him as the Messiah, they know he has a reputation for wise, compassionate teachings and for good deeds and miracles. They find it difficult to deny he seems to be a holy man, even as they think his teachings are unusual, and in their view, run counter to Jewish traditions and even Jewish law.

The second reason they want Pilate's approval is Jews needed Roman approval to subject anyone to death by crucifixion. Crucifixion was Rome's most torturous form of execution and they used it enthusiastically. Here's one example: years after Jesus' death, when the Roman General Titus besieged Jerusalem and its inhabitants were starving, some snuck out of the city's gates to forage for food. Many of these people would be caught – on some days Titus' soldiers caught as many as 500 – and the enraged Roman soldiers would nail them to crosses. So many were crucified that the Romans ran out of room for crosses and ran out of wood to crucify the desperate and starving Jews attempting to escape their doomed city.

Yet it seems Jews did not seek Roman approval to stone to death one lawbreaker. Remember the woman caught in adultery? Jews were ready to stone her without Roman approval. Remember too when Jesus said in the Temple, "The Father and I are one," (John 9:30) and his enemies picked up stones to kill him. Remember also when Stephen was brought before the Council and he was falsely accused, and Stephen's opponents "began stoning him." (Acts 7:58 NASB)

But Jewish authorities did not want Jesus stoned to death, but crucified. Why? I think Deuteronomy (21:22-23) gives the answer:

> When someone is convicted of a capital offense and is put to death, and you hang him on a gibbet, his body must not remain there overnight; it must be buried on the same day. Anyone hanged is accursed in the sight of God, and the land which the Lord your God is giving you as your holding must not be polluted.

Crucifixion meant the person died under a curse. Jewish religious leaders wanted a public execution so the people could see the man who said he was the Son of God as accursed.

The need to share blame, the need for an approved crucifixion, and the need to indicate the victim was accursed. It was for these reasons the religious leaders wanted to crucify Jesus of Nazareth. While we can logically consider these reasons, we can only partially understand why the Divine decided that the painful path of insult, rejection, and death for His Son was necessary to restore peace between humans and their Creator.

In many places and many times, Jews have suffered insult and death from Christians who blame them for the death of Jesus of Nazareth. Should their ancestor's role in the death of Jesus be taught? Shouldn't caution be exercised in mentioning it?

We should teach the truth. The religious leaders at that time conspired to kill Jesus of Nazareth and that is fact. The Gentile leaders of the time did not stop the execution, and, moreover, authorized it and carried it out. That is also fact.

Christians have warred on Jews and on other Christians. It is accurate to say that because of the unchristian behavior of Christians the name Jesus does not symbolize love and peace to many Jews, but rather for many Jews it means hostility and hatred. I think we can agree that this is not what Jesus of Nazareth wanted his name to symbolize to his fellow Jews or anyone else.

For those who accept the New Testament and yet continue to hold animus toward Jews, I point to the words of the Prophet Ezekiel (18:20 NASB)

> **The person who sins will die. The son will not bear the punishment for the father's iniquity, nor will the father bear the punishment for the son's iniquity; the righteousness of the righteous will be upon himself, and the wickedness of the wicked will be upon himself.**

If a son is not guilty for his father's sins, how then are Jews still guilty of something their ancestors did 2,000 years ago?

Still, some Christians may think that killing the Messiah is the ultimate crime and cannot be forgiven. For any who think this, it is good to recall what Jesus said at his crucifixion:

> **Father, forgive them; for they do not know what they are doing.**
>
> **(Luke 23:34 NASB)**

47 Tell me, Simon, from whom do earthly monarchs collect tribute money?

Matthew 17:25

> **"Tell me, Simon, from whom do earthly monarchs collect tribute money? From their own people, or from aliens?" "From aliens," said Peter. "Yes," said Jesus, "and their own people are exempt. But as we do not want to cause offence, go and cast a line in the lake; take the first fish you catch, open its mouth, and you will find a silver coin; take that and pay the tax for us both."**
>
> **Matthew 17:25-27**

Capernaum tax collectors were collecting for the Temple's upkeep when they cornered Simon Peter and asked, "Does your master not pay temple tax?" Peter replies, "He does," then he goes to see Jesus, but before Peter can speak, Jesus asks, **"Tell me, Simon, from whom do earthly monarchs collect tribute money? From their own** people, or from aliens?" "From aliens," said Peter. "Yes," said Jesus, "and their own people are exempt."

Two miracles occur here: one is Jesus knew of Peter's conversation with the tax collectors before Peter told him of it. (By the way, the tax was high, equaling two days pay.) The second miracle was the method Jesus used to provide the tax money – by telling Peter to fish for it. Note that Jesus' question to Peter implies his followers are people of God and not aliens, and therefore exempt from paying the tax. But Jesus does not want to offend so he supplies the tax by having Peter find a silver coin in the mouth of a fish.

Compared to other miracles, these are minor and do not involve feeding thousands or giving sight to the blind. They are unseen by crowds or even other disciples, but they show us that God assists us when assistance is needed, and sometimes in ways too small for the world to see.

And something else here – did you notice Peter's greater faith? When Jesus first met Peter (then Simon), Jesus asked him to sail in deeper waters and fish again, but Peter challenged Jesus' request because he had fished all day and caught nothing. But then Peter does try again, and his catch is so massive that other fishermen must help him to bring it in. But this time, when Jesus asks Peter to cast a line and pluck a coin from the mouth of the first fish he catches, Peter does not hesitate. This time Peter simply believes.

> 48 If one of you has a hundred sheep and loses one of them, does he not leave the ninety-nine in the wilderness and go after the one that is missing until he finds it?
>
> **Luke 15:4**

If one of you has a hundred sheep and loses one of them, does he not leave the ninety-nine in the wilderness and go after the one that is missing until he finds it? And when he does, he lifts it joyfully on his shoulders, and goes home to call his friends and neighbors together. "Rejoice with me!" he cries. "I have found my lost sheep." In the same way, I tell you, there will be greater joy in heaven over one sinner who repents than over ninety-nine righteous people who do not need to repent.

Or again, if a woman has ten silver coins and loses one of them, does she not light the lamp, sweep out the house, and look in every corner until she finds it? And when she does, she calls her friends and neighbors together, and says, "Rejoice with me! I have found the coin that I have lost." In the same way, I tell you, there is joy among the angels of God over one sinner who repents.

Luke 15:4-10

Some business people might view the "lost sheep" parable as unrealistic and say, "If I own 100 sheep, horses or cows, and I lose one, that may be sub-optimal, but it is the cost of doing business, and I can still make a nice profit on the other 99."

But humans do not reason like God. God is not interested in profits but in everything He created.

When some Christians hear atheists insult God, these Christians are tempted to think the atheist's hatred deserves divine punishment, but the Lost Sheep parable tells us God wants everyone to know the truth, whether they are smart or simple-minded, agnostic or atheist. No one is beyond the power of God, although, it seems that some are very far away from that power, still, all things are possible with God.

I tell you, there will be rejoicing among the angels of God over one sinner who repents.

Luke 15:10

For the Son of Man has come to seek and to save that which was lost.

Luke 19:10 (NASB)

49 You scoundrel! I cancelled the whole of your debt when you appealed to me; ought you not to have shown mercy to your fellow-servant just as I showed mercy to you?

Matthew 18:32-33

Then he sent for the man and said, "You scoundrel! I cancelled the whole of your debt when you appealed to me; ought you not to have shown mercy to your fellow-servant just as I showed mercy to you?" And so angry was the master that he condemned the man to be tortured until he should pay the debt in full. That is how my heavenly Father will deal with you, unless you each forgive your brother from your hearts.

Matthew 18:32-35

The servant owed his king 15 years worth of salary! When the servant could not repay the massive debt, the king ordered the man, his wife, children, and everything he owned to be sold to help meet his debts. The servant begged for time to pay, "Be patient with me and I will pay you in full." The big-hearted king not only let the man go but also cancelled all of the man's debt.

As soon as this servant left, he ran into a fellow-servant who owed him one day's wage, and he grabbed the man by the throat and demanded payment. The man begged for time to repay, "Be patient with me and I will repay you." The first servant wouldn't listen and had his fellow-servant thrown in jail. When the king heard of this he ordered the first servant brought back to him, and said:

> **"You scoundrel! I cancelled the whole of your debt when you appealed to me; ought you not to have shown mercy to your fellow-servant just as I showed mercy to you?"**

Understand the principle revealed here and you will understand a leading precept taught by the Messiah – the principle of Divine Reciprocity. Understand this and you will also learn how Christianity differs from other world religions.

I earlier said it is more difficult to be a Christian than to be an adherent of any other faith or philosophy, but it is simpler to be a Christian than to be an adherent of most other religions or philosophies. The difficult aspect of being a Christian is that Jesus taught followers to be perfect as God is perfect, and that is an undeniably difficult goal.

Yet it is simpler to be a Christian because Christians are not required to make a pilgrimage to a certain location, or to worship on a specific mountain, or to sacrifice animals in rituals, or to wear particular clothing. Nor do followers of the Messiah need to remember a list of laws. Christians can eat any food cooked in any manner –French, Chinese, Italian, or American. It does not matter. All the requirements found in other religions are unnecessary for the Christian and the Christian needs no temple because the Christian is the Temple.

The requirements for followers of the Messiah are: accept Jesus of Nazareth is the Son of God and everything that recognition signifies, and grant reciprocity to fellow servants; granting to others what the Christian has been granted – pardon.

Simple but difficult.

> You, therefore, must be perfect, as your heavenly Father is perfect.
>
> **Matthew 5:48 (RSV)**

50 Have you never read that in the beginning the Creator made them male and female?

Matthew 19:4

Some Pharisees came and tested him by asking, "Is it lawful for a man to divorce his wife for any cause he pleases?" He responded by asking, "Have you never read that in the beginning the Creator made them male and female?" and he added, "This is why a man leaves his father and his mother, and is united to his wife, and the two become one flesh. It follows that they are no longer two individuals: they are one flesh. Therefore, what God has joined together, man must not separate."

Matthew 19:3-6

We know about important commitments: vows to God; allegiance to one's nation; words of honor; and oaths of perpetual bonds, and like these solemn matters, Jesus calls marriage an enduring vow linking man and woman through life.

The Pharisees make a counterpoint and ask Jesus why Moses allowed divorce, Jesus then questions their knowledge of God's original intent, **"Have you never read that in the beginning the Creator made them male and female?"** and Jesus told the Pharisees that Moses only compromised on marriage and divorce because of their obstinate nature. Jesus appears to recognize one exception:

> **but I say to you that everyone who divorces his wife, except for *the* reason of unchastity, makes her commit adultery; and whoever marries a divorced woman commits adultery.**
>
> **Matthew 5:32 (NASB)**

Jesus taught marriage was originally meant to be a life-long bond and wanted to restore that perspective to his fellow Jews. During Jesus' life, Jews followed the Law, which stipulated that divorce was legal. Moses' Law understood marriage as a legal obligation; Jesus said marriage is a standard in the heart, and taught: "You have heard that they were told, 'Do not commit adultery.' But what I tell you is this: If a man looks at a woman with a lustful eye, he has already committed adultery with her in his heart."

Jesus taught a higher standard, yet we remember when Jesus was asked to pass judgment on a woman caught in adultery, his reply to her accusers saved her from being stoned. We comprehend how advanced the teachings of Jesus are when we hear today of women in the Middle East being stoned to death for one offense or another. Jesus taught against adultery in fact and in the heart. He rejected stoning. We see the teachings of Jesus continue to challenge our world even 2,000 years after he taught them.

51 Why do you call Me good? No one is good except God alone.

Mark 10:18 (NASB)

> As He was setting out on a journey, a man ran up to Him and knelt before Him, and asked Him, "Good Teacher, what shall I do to inherit eternal life?" And Jesus said to him, "Why do you call Me good? No one is good except God alone."
>
> **Mark 10:17-18 (NASB)**
> **also Matthew 19:17 and Luke 18:19**

When someone calls Jesus "good," Jesus responds with a question, **"Why do you call Me good?"**

The Messiah did not consider himself equal to the God, as we know from Philippians 2:6: "He was in the form of God; yet he laid no claim to equality with God." And Jesus knew what the God of Israel said to Moses, "Do not make anything to rank with me; neither gods of silver nor gods of gold shall you make for yourselves." (Exodus 20:23 NAB)

We often call many things "good" – a car, a movie, a cup of coffee, or just the weather. And we also call some people "good," but Jesus of Nazareth, the Messiah, God's son, rejects the word "good" being applied to him because he knows God alone is good. It is worth remembering what Jesus thought and taught concerning the word "good".

52 What is written in the law? What is your reading of it?

Luke 10:26

> A lawyer once came forward to test him by asking: "Teacher, what must I do to inherit eternal life?" Jesus said, "What is written in the law? What is your reading of it?" He replied, "Love the Lord your God with all your heart, and with all your soul, with all you strength, and with all your mind; and your neighbor as yourself." "That is the right answer," said Jesus; "do that and you will have life."
> **Luke 10:25-28**

Jesus responds to the lawyer's question with a question, asking him how he interprets the law: "What is your reading of it?" The lawyer wisely identifies the heart of the law:

> **"Love the Lord your God with all your heart, and with all your soul, with all your strength, and with all your mind; and your neighbor as yourself."**

Is it possible that all the Psalms, prophets, Gospels, Paul's writings, and in fact all the books of the Bible are encapsulated in the 28 words the lawyer spoke to Jesus? Yes, it is.

Jesus told the lawyer, "That is the right answer, do that and you will have life."

The Messiah taught the Law has a hierarchy and that there is a facet of the Law that is most important and ranks highest.

Here is a story about two rabbis.

Hillel and Shammai were great rabbis and moral leaders. Both Hillel and Shammai were born before Jesus (Hillel may have lived at the same time of Jesus, but if he did, he would have been very old when Jesus was a boy). Both Hillel and Shammai were experts in the Law, but they differed how they thought the law should be applied. Shammai thought the Law must be applied firmly; while Hillel thought understanding the heart of the Law was more important. The two rabbis also differed in disposition, with Shammai being hospitable, yet quick-tempered, while Hillel was unflappable and even-tempered.

This story about Hillel and Shammai involves a pagan who challenged Shammai that he would become a Jew if Shammai could teach him the entire Torah while the man stood on one foot. A ridiculous challenge when one remembers rabbis and scribes spent their lives studying the Torah and the law. Shammai is irritated by the man's ludicrous challenge and sends him away.

The pagan then goes to Hillel and makes the same challenge, and Hillel tells him, "Whatever is hateful to you, don't do to others, this is the whole Law, the rest is mere commentary."

Hillel's answer to the man foreshadows Jesus' response to the lawyer about what is indispensible for life. While Jesus' answer is more positive, it has a clear proximity to Hillel's answer. And why shouldn't it? Jesus knew Torah, the prophets, and very likely the teachings of the Jewish rabbis, of which Hillel was one.

We see Hillel's influence later in the Bible when Paul wrote he was strictly educated in ancestral law by Gamaliel. Gamaliel was Hillel's grandson and he is the same man who advocated a wise and peaceful attitude toward the Apostles (see Acts 5:34-42).

(Note: Jesus in Mark 12:28-34 has a conversation with a scribe that is similar to the conversation he had with the lawyer.)

53 Why be jealous because I am generous?
Matthew 20:15

When it was the turn of the men who had come first, they expected something extra, but were paid the same as the others. As they took it, they grumbled at their employer: "These latecomers did only one hour's work, yet you have treated them on a level with us, who have sweated the whole day long in the blazing sun!" The owner turned to one of them and said, "My friend, I am not being unfair to you. You agreed on the usual wage for the day, did you not? Take your pay and go home. I choose to give the last man the same as you. Surely I am free to do what I like with my own money? Why be jealous because I am generous?" So the last will be first and the first last.

Matthew 20:10-16

In heaven, there may be some ancient Israelites watching as non-Jews arrive in the Kingdom, and say, "See these Gentiles enter the kingdom and receive the same reward we were given, even though they are not descendants of Abraham. Is it fair these Gentiles receive the same reward as we Jews who suffered for being chosen by God? Is that fair?"

In heaven, there may be a community of early Christians watching the arrival of modern Christians, and say, "We early Christians suffered persecution – and many were tortured and died for following Jesus. But look at these Christians who had soft lives and never suffered as Christians, but they are given mansions in heaven just as we are! Is that fair?"

Perhaps we ourselves will be in the Kingdom and see some arriving and say, "See that man? He was immoral all his whole life and became a Christian only a few days before he died – yet he is in heaven and given rewards like us, even though we lived our lives struggling to be Christian. Is that fair?"

If people say such things in heaven, what are we to we think of that perspective? One well-known Christian wrote this:

> "… what a strange attitude … It seems as if we want to be rewarded, not just with our own salvation, but most especially with other people's damnation … Anyone who looks on the loss of salvation for others as the condition … on which he serves Christ will in the end only be able to turn away grumbling, because *that* kind of reward is contrary to the loving-kindness of God."[6]

"Why be jealous because I am generous?"

God is generous with everyone. God is generous with you.

---

[6] Joseph Cardinal Ratzinger (Pope Emeritus Benedict XVI), *What It Means to Be a Christian* (San Francisco: Ignatius Press, 2006), Page 49. www.ignatius.com. Used with permission.

54 What is it you want?
Matthew 20:21

You do not understand what you are asking. Can you drink the cup that I am to drink?
Matthew 20:22

The mother of Zebedee's sons then approached him with her sons. She bowed before him and begged a favour. "What is it you want?" asked Jesus. She replied, "Give orders that in your kingdom these two sons of mine may sit next to you, one at your right hand and the other at your left." Jesus turned to the brothers and said, "You do not understand what you are asking. Can you drink the cup that I am to drink?" "We can," they replied. "You shall indeed drink my cup," he said; "but to sit on my right or on my left is not for me to grant; that honour is for those to whom it has already been assigned by my Father."

Matthew 20:20-23

This story is reported in Matthew, Mark, and Luke, with the narration woven a bit differently in each Gospel, but they share this identical question: who is truly great?

As they travel through the Galilee, Mark reports Jesus notices the disciples arguing and asks them what their dispute is about. Nothing, they say, but in actual fact, they had been arguing over who is the greatest disciple. Jesus stops, he sits down and tells his men to gather around, and then tells them (in my own loose translation): You know who is the greatest? It is the one who is the least and serves the most.

We may find Matthew's version a bit amusing, as we are familiar with the pride of mothers, who always see their own child as the best and brightest, always believing their child superior in intelligence and attractiveness. So we are not surprised when the mother of James and John goes to Jesus and begs him that her sons sit on his right and left when he comes into his kingdom.

This may be the most audacious request Jesus has heard, but he does not criticize the mother making it, rather he places her request in a serious perspective. Turning to her sons, Jesus said, **"You do not understand what you are asking. Can you drink the cup that I am to drink?"** Which is to say, are you willing to face what I must face? They answer yes. Very well, Jesus says, you will experience it, but as for your mother's request, **"That honour is for those to whom it has already been assigned by my Father."** In saying, "to whom it has already been assigned," Jesus reminds us that the future is obscure to us, but the God of Israel knows all.

The other disciples are irritated at the mother's appeal, but Jesus corrects their perspective, telling them in heaven the greatest serve the most, and in fact, he himself did not come to earth to be served but to serve.

This should not have surprised the disciples because God used the word "servants" for many of their ancestors.

God told Isaac: "I will bless you, and multiply your descendents, For the sake of My **servant** Abraham. (Genesis 26:24 NASB). Elijah was called the Lord's **servant** in Second Kings (9:36), and the prophet Daniel (Daniel 9:17) called himself a **servant**, and Isaiah was called a **servant** by God in (Isaiah 20:3). Joshua, too, is called the **servant** of the Lord (Joshua 24:29) and Moses (Exodus 14:31) and David (Psalm

36) are called **servants** of God. And Isaiah speaks of a suffering **servant** (53:10).

The disciples should have guessed the greatest among them would be the greatest servant. We know of humanitarians and holy people who lead lives of service to others. One Italian monk who lived in the last century became known for his holiness and miracle cures of the sick. When he was old and nearing his death, he told his fellow monks that his real work would begin after he died. This monk knew those closest to God are called to greater service in the next life.

55 What do want Me to do for you?
Matthew 20:32 (NASB)

> And Jesus stopped and called them, and said, "What do want Me to do for you?" They said to Him, "Lord, *we want* our eyes to be opened." Moved with compassion, Jesus touched their eyes; and immediately they regained their sight and followed Him.
>
> **Matthew 20:32-34 (NASB)**

How many solicitations do you receive by mail every week? How many requests for donations? How many government requests for information? How many requests do you get at work? How many emails?

Yet the Son of God asks for nothing from the man near Jericho (who is identified as Bartimaeus in Mark), instead, Jesus asked the man what *he* wanted – as though Jesus were his servant.

Bartimaeus said, "Rabbi, I want my sight back." God is generous and in His generosity sent His son to serve and to save humanity. Notice after the man makes his request, Jesus says, **"Go; your faith has made you well." (Mark 10:52 NASB)** *Faith is acceptance of a request made in faith.*

Notice that when Bartimaeus yells, "Jesus, Son of David, have mercy on me!" The crowd tells him to be quiet, but Bartimaeus only shouts louder, "Son of David, have mercy on me!" (Mark 10:47-48 NASB)

When you want God's attention, some people may not want to hear you, but God does.

> **And answering him, Jesus said "What do you want Me to do for you?"**
> **Mark 10:51 (NASB)**

> **"What do you want Me to do for you?"**
> **Luke 18:41 (NASB)**

> **Note: In Matthew's report of this event, there are two blind men, who, after receiving their sight, follow Jesus.**

56 Are there not twelve hours in the day?
John 11:9 (NASB)

Jesus answered, "Are there not twelve hours in the day? If anyone walks in the day, he does not stumble, because he sees the light of this world. But

> **if anyone walks in the night, he stumbles, because the light is not in him."**
>
> **John 11:9-10 (NASB)**

Jesus' question seems a little odd, but less so if we remember some of his other statements in John.

> **We must work the works of Him who sent Me as long as it is day; night is coming when no one can work. While I am in the world I am the Light of the world.**
>
> **John 9:4-5 (NASB)**

> **I am the Light of the world; he who follows Me will not walk in the darkness, but will have the Light of life.**
>
> **John 8:12 (NASB)**

> **I have come *as* Light into the world, so that everyone who believes in Me will not remain in darkness.**
>
> **John 12:46 (NASB)**

God and Jesus and light are clearly linked. And light is such a cardinal Biblical element that it appears in the third sentence of the entire Bible:

> **Then God said, "Let there be light"; and there was light. God saw that the light was good; and God separated the light from darkness."**
>
> **Genesis 1:3-4 (NASB)**

In the first book of the Bible, Genesis begins with the division of light and darkness, while the Bible's last book, Revelation, ends with light in the New Jerusalem.

And the city has no need of the sun or of the moon
to shine on it, for the glory of God has illumined
it, and its lamp *is* the lamb."

Revelation 21:23 (NASB)

That single phrase in Genesis describes all human history – **God
saw that the light was good; and God separated the light from
darkness.** History is the process of separating light from darkness,
of separating the children of light from the children of darkness. We
now live in light and darkness, a long-term amalgam that will end
and then we will live in the Kingdom of Heaven, a kingdom of light.

**The nations will walk by its light, and the kings
of the earth will bring their glory into it. In the
daytime (for there will be no night there) its gates
will never be closed**

Revelation 21:24-25 (NASB)

57 Was the baptism of John from Heaven or from men?

Luke 20:4 (NASB)

Jesus answered and said to them, "I will also ask
you a question, and you tell Me: was the baptism
of John from Heaven or from men?"

Luke 20:3-4 (NASB)

What did you go out into the wilderness to see? A
reed shaken by the wind?

> **But what did you go out to see? A man dressed in soft clothing? Those who are splendidly clothed and live in luxury are *found* in royal palaces! But what did you go out to see? A prophet? Yes, I say to you, and one who is more than a prophet.**
>
> **Luke 7:24-26 (NASB)**

The scribes, elders, and chief priests ask Jesus about the origin of his authority, but first Jesus wants them to answer his question whether the baptism was from God or man.

Jesus' opponents decide they are trapped, because if they say John's baptism was from God, Jesus will say, "Why didn't you believe him?" but if they say, "From men," then the people will stone them because the people are convinced John was a prophet, so the religious experts told Jesus that they could not tell. So they do not answer and neither does Jesus answer their question.

Jesus uses John the Baptist to test the understanding of his fellow Jews, as we read in Luke 7:24-26 above. However, I think this is the most striking verse in Luke's Chapter 7:

> **I say to you, among those born of women there is no one greater than John; yet he who is least in the kingdom of God is greater than he.**
>
> **Luke 7:28 (NASB)**

Jesus teaches magnitudes of difference beyond what we understand in our limited reality, where people categorize differences in temperature, the horsepower of engines, and grades of coffee. The Messiah categorizes the differences of ultimate things. Thus the Messiah has the divine wisdom to categorize John the Baptist as greater than anyone born on earth, and then he also says that even *the least* in the Kingdom of God is greater than the Baptist – an amazing thought when we consider that we are called to enter that Kingdom.

The difference between our world and the next cannot be comprehended. Paul wrote of the gulf between our world and the next: "Scripture speaks of 'things beyond our seeing, things beyond our hearing, things beyond our imaging, all prepared by God for those who love him.'"

1 Corinthians 2:9

58 But what do you think?
Matthew 21:28 (NASB)

"But what do you think? A man who had two sons, and he came to the first and said, 'Son, go to work today in the vineyard.' And he answered, 'I will not'; but afterwards he regretted it and went. The man came to the second and said the same thing; and he answered, 'I *will*, sir'; but he did not go. Which of the two did the will of his father? They said, 'The first.' Jesus said to them, Truly, I say to you that the tax collectors and prostitutes will get into the kingdom of God before you. For John came to you in the kingdom of righteousness and you did not believe him; but the tax collectors and prostitutes did believe him; and you, seeing *this*, did not even feel remorse afterward so as to believe him."

Matthew 21:28-32 (NASB)

Jesus' question, "Which of the two did what his father wanted?" reaffirms the superiority of actions over words. We can see God does not judge by our promises but by our actions and the intensions of our hearts:

God *sees* not as man sees, for man looks at the outward appearance, but the Lord looks at the heart.

1 Samuel 16:7 (NASB)

59 But Jesus looked at them and said, "What then is this that is written: 'THE STONE WHICH THE BUILDERS REJECTED, THIS BECAME THE CHIEF CORNER *STONE*"?

Luke 20:17 (NASB)

The owner of the vineyard said, "What shall I do? I will send my beloved son; perhaps they will respect him." But when the vine-growers saw him, they reasoned with one another, saying, "This is the heir; let us kill him so that the inheritance will be ours." So they threw him out of the vineyard and killed him. What, then, will the owner of the vineyard do to them? He will come and destroy these vine-growers and give the vineyard to others."

When they heard it, they said, "May it never be!" But Jesus looked at them and said, "What then is this that is written: 'THE STONE WHICH THE BUILDERS REJECTED, THIS BECAME THE CHIEF CORNER *STONE*'?

Everyone who falls on that stone will be broken to pieces; but on whomever it falls, it will scatter him like dust."

The scribes and chief priests tried to lay hands on him that very hour, and they feared the people; for they understood that He spoke this parable against them.

Luke 20:13-19 (NASB)

Jesus "looked straight at them" and said, "He will come and put those tenants to death and give the vineyard to others."

Why did the scribes and chief priests immediately recognize the parable was aimed at them? Because they knew the Jewish nation is symbolically linked with vineyards in the Bible.

Jesus used images that his fellow Jews will quickly understand, like planting and harvesting, the rights of kings, managing vineyards, and the accountability of workers. Jesus especially liked the image of the vine:

I am the vine; you are the branches; he who abides in Me and I in him, he bears much fruit, for apart from Me you can do nothing. If anyone does not abide in Me, he is thrown away as a branch and dries up; and they gather them, and they cast them into the fire and they are burned.

John 15:5-6 (NASB)

While millions of people sincerely search for truth, many of these same people ignore the Bible, which is the Word of God. For many, the Bible remains an unexamined and mysterious book, even among some who are themselves Christians.

Many truth-seekers do not accept how a good God would permit anyone to suffer eternal punishment, but that is a misunderstanding, because God does not want anyone to suffer punishment. God does, however, permit people to suffer the consequences of their own deeds, of their own disbelief, and their own rejection God's Word. No one is forced into the Kingdom of God. John 15:5-6 makes it clear that people who deny the truth taught by the Messiah are rejecting the truth that they were born to understand.

> 60 "My friend," said the king, "how do you come to be here without wedding clothes? But he had nothing to say.
>
> **Matthew 22:12**

When the king came in to watch them feasting, he observed a man who was not dressed for a wedding. "My friend," said the king, "how do you come to be here without wedding clothes?" But he had nothing to say.

Matthew 22:11-12

Perhaps some of us have seen an improperly attired wedding guest, but none of us have seen this happen at a wedding: the host orders a guest tied hand-and-foot and thrown into darkness where there is weeping, screams, and darkness. Remember this parable is about a royal wedding, where the king himself ensures the wedding banquet is going well, and that every guest is appropriately dressed for the event, which is a royal wedding more spectacular than even the British public has ever seen.

Context is important in this parable and you should read it in Matthew's 22nd chapter. My abbreviated version of Matthews 22nd Chapter, verses 1-14, follows.

Jesus begins his parable by saying, "The kingdom of heaven is like this," and describes a king's wedding feast for his son. The monarch is enthusiastic for the guests to join the celebration, and sends royal servants off to the invited guests, but the invitees brush off the invitation snubbing the king's servants. The king does not give up, and again sends servants to the invitees, "Everything is ready! Come to the wedding," and again the royal invitation is declined and the invited return to their daily work; but worse, some of the invited guests not only reject the king's royal invitation, but kill the king's servants who were sent to invite them.

The king is enraged at the rude, insolvent and violent behavior of the invitees, so he does not send more of his servants, but instead his army to the city where the invited guests live and orders his army to burn the city and destroy its inhabitants.

The king said the original guests were unworthy of the honor of attending the wedding banquet and issues new instructions to his servants: the magnificent banquet remains ready, now servants must go to the main roads and invite everyone – good and bad alike. Thus did the servants do and thus was the wedding hall finally filled with guests. The king reviewed his son's wedding celebration, but when he does, he notices one man completely unsuited for the event and asks him for an explanation, but the man has no answer and the king orders him expelled from the celebration into the darkness outside.

There is more than one interpretation possible for this parable, and this is mine, which has not been approved by the Pope, the Archbishop of Canterbury, or any other religious leader.

In the parable, the king is God in Heaven and the wedding is for Jesus of Nazareth. The original invited guests are the 12 tribes of Israel who generally declined the invitation to the Son's wedding celebration. The king's royal servants are God's prophets who proclaim the Lord's invitation to the celebration, which is the Kingdom of God, but the invitation is spurned and God's servants – the prophets – are rejected and killed. The king (the Lord) is infuriated at the treatment of his servants-prophets and orders the destruction of the city where his prophets were killed. The city of Jerusalem.

Jesus' parable carried a prophecy: 40 years after Jesus was crucified in Jerusalem the Roman Imperial Army surrounded that city, starved the people, burned Jerusalem to the ground, and annihilated hundreds of thousands of Jews. The survivors were brought to Rome, paraded through the streets in chains in a victory celebration over the rebellious province, then the Jewish prisoners were sold as slaves. The Arch of Titus memorializing Rome's conquest over Israel still stands in Rome today and the "Wailing Wall" in Jerusalem is a remnant of the retaining wall that once surrounded the Temple Mount. Israelis and Jews from every nation pray at the Wailing Wall and lament the destruction of the Temple, which after nearly 20 centuries has never been rebuilt.

Now back to wedding parable: when the king decided to expand his invitation to his son's wedding to every nation – Jew or Gentile – many accepted and attended the wedding banquet, but they are unable to stay at the wedding celebration without proper dress, which is: a life lived according to the teachings of the groom – the king's son, Jesus of Nazareth.

Now some Christians might say, "I disagree with that interpretation, because once a person accepts Jesus in faith, nothing further is required, you are welcomed into the Kingdom of God." Perhaps they are right. As I said, different interpretations are possible. Mine differs because I note the man in the parable is allowed into the celebration and is apparently enjoying the wedding celebration until the king sees that he is not dressed for the occasion. So it is the king, the Lord alone, with perfect judgment, who decides who is welcome at the wedding and may stay at the celebration and who is not welcome.

Again, many Christians say one's faith is the required attire and that the man in the parable who is thrown into darkness suffered that fate because he was not attired with faith in Jesus. Such an interpretation may be correct, but the fact the man had already been at the heavenly wedding says to my thinking that this is what Jesus meant at the end of this parable when he said, "Many are invited, but few are chosen."

At the end of life one faces individual judgment, and then at a further point in the future, I believe there is a second and final judgment at the resurrection, which is the general judgment of all humans that will take place when God Almighty will verify the first individual judgment.

The royal wedding is a profound parable.

> 61 "Why are you trying to catch me out? Show me the coin used for the tax." They handed him a silver piece. Jesus asked, "Whose head is this, and whose inscription?"
>
> **Matthew 22:18-20**

"Give us your ruling on this: are we or are we not permitted to pay taxes to the Roman emperor?" Jesus was aware of their malicious intention and said, "You hypocrites! Why are you trying to catch me out? Show me the coin used for the tax." They handed him a silver piece. Jesus asked, "Whose head is this, and whose inscription?" "Caesar's," they replied. He said to them, "Then pay to Caesar what belongs to Caesar, and to God what belongs to God."

Matthew 22:17-21

Three Gospels – Matthew, Mark (12:13-17), and Luke (20:20-26) all report this famous encounter between Jesus and the Pharisees.

Some Pharisees and supporters of Herod's party want to trap Jesus, so they dream up a question that is so devious that any answer Jesus gives will alienate Jewish nationalists, who hate Rome's taxes, or identify Jesus as Caesar's enemy.

So they find Jesus, pose as admirers of Jesus and offer him insincere praise before ambushing him with a question: Should Jews pay Caesar taxes or not?

Jesus does not seem to carry coins with him, because before responding, he asks to be shown the coin used for the tax. He was probably given a denarius, which we assume Jesus quickly examined, handed back, and then asked Pharisees two specific questions:

"Whose head is this, and whose inscription?"

"Caesar's," they respond.

"Then pay to Caesar what belongs to Caesar, and to God what belongs to God."

Jesus' answer altered the course of world history, because after hearing it Christians know it is not necessary to live under a Christian government. For Christians the government is naturally important, but as they already live under God's law, they do not seek a religious government. Christians can live under God's laws anywhere as long as the government that they live under does not hinder, penalize, or otherwise jeopardize or threaten Christian lives.

Christians seek a government to protect their rights and the rights of all believers, and even those with no belief, as they may be persuaded to the truth with the truth.

126

Should, however, any government attempt to insert its power between Christians and their consciences, or make an effort to force Christians to choose between a king and the Christ, Christians will choose the King of Kings. The followers of the Messiah will not place man before God. They will refuse allegiance to a false god.

Still, by this answer of Jesus to the Pharisees, Christians understand that they could live under any government, whether run by Socialists who seek high taxes and more government regulations and ownership, or by Libertarians who dislike taxes and government regulations, or if the government is run by agnostics or by even atheists. Regarding the government they live under, the foremost question for Christians is their right to acknowledge the Supreme God and Jesus of Nazareth without penalty or prejudice.

> **62 As for the resurrection of the dead, have you never read what God himself said to you: "I am the God of Abraham, the God of Isaac, the God of Jacob"?**
> **Matthew 22:31-32**

At the resurrection, then, whose wife will she be, since they had all married her? Jesus answered: "How far you are from the truth! You know neither the scriptures nor the power of God. In the resurrection men and women do not marry; they are like angels in heaven.

"As for the resurrection of the dead, have you never read what God himself said to you: 'I am the God of Abraham, the God of Isaac, the God of Jacob'?

**God is not the God of the dead but of the living."
When the crowds heard this, they were amazed at
his teaching.**

**Matthew 22:28-33
Also Mark 12:18-27 and Luke 20:27-40**

The Sadducees were a leading religious faction who doubted the resurrection of the dead, and they posed a question to Jesus that they thought he could not answer about a woman who had been married seven times to seven different men, and in succession, each husband had died, and then finally the woman herself died. In this case, the Sadducees ask, which man would be her husband at the resurrection? The wisdom of Jesus replied.

> **How far you are from the truth! You know neither the scriptures nor the power of God. In the resurrection men and women do not marry; they are like angels in heaven.**
>
> **As for the resurrection of the dead, have you never read what God himself said to you: 'I am the God of Abraham, the God of Isaac, the God of Jacob'? God is not the God of the dead but of the living.**

Sadducees do not understand God's Word or God's power, which requires grace from God.

Science tells us if we sit motionless in a chair, in reality, we are spinning with the Earth at 700 miles per hour. And at the same time, Earth is orbiting the Sun at 67,000 miles an hour. Also at the same time, the entire Solar System, including Earth, moves around our Galaxy at 550,000 miles an hour. And the Galaxy itself moves through the universe at over a million miles an hour. So the Earth spins on its axis, while orbiting the Sun, while the Sun swirls around the Galaxy, and the Galaxy itself travels through the universe – motion within motion, within faster motion, within yet faster motion, all undetectable to our senses.

The Earth is huge and we may not personally know a single person who has travelled around it, but relative to our Sun, the Earth is small, so small compared to the Sun that it would require 109 Earth-sized planets, placed side by side, to stretch across the diameter of the Sun and the Sun is more than a million times the volume of our planet Earth. Then again, the Sun itself is tiny when compared to the Red Giant stars, which are 100 times bigger in diameter than our Sun and 10,000 times wider than our Earth.

These massive magnitudes help us appreciate our insignificance in God's universe, but when Jesus tells the Sadducees, **You know neither the scriptures nor the power of God**, he does not mean they are ignorant of the sun, moon or stars that they see, but that they do not recognize the power of God, who they cannot see. The Sadducees seem to have forgotten the God who inspired a shepherd to say to an armor-clad, nine-foot giant, "I come against you in the name of the Lord of hosts, the God of the armies of Israel, whom you have taunted." (1 Samuel 17:45 NASB) Sadducees seem to have forgotten the power of God who listened to Elijah's plea to return a widow's son to life. (see 1 Kings 17:22) The Sadducees had forgotten the power of God who healed a Roman centurion's servant at a distance, with Jesus telling the Roman, "Go; it shall be done for you as you have believed." (Matthew 8:13 NASB) Thus, they knew neither the scriptures nor the power of God.

> 63 Then He said to them, "How *is it that* they say the Christ is David's son?
> Luke 20:41 (NASB)

Then He said to them, "How *is it that* they say the Christ is David's son? For David himself says in the Book of Psalms: 'The Lord said to my Lord, "Sit at my right hand until I make your enemies a footstool for your feet." Therefore David calls him 'Lord,' and how is He his son?"

Luke 20:41-44 (NASB)
See also Matthew 22:41-46

My translation:

Jesus: Can I ask you a question?

Pharisees: Yes.

Jesus: The Messiah, whose son will he be?

Pharisees: David's son.

Jesus: Right, then tell me why David, under the inspiration of the Holy Spirit, said: "The Lord said to my Lord."? If David calls the Messiah "Lord", how can the Messiah be his son?

Pharisees: (silence.)

Jesus questioned the Pharisees regarding David being the ancestor of the Messiah, because if that were so, why would David call the Messiah "his Lord"? After all, isn't a son subordinate to his father? Yet, David called his son (the Messiah) "Lord" as though David were subordinate to his own son.

Although the Messiah is indeed David's son through heritage, he is superior to his earthly father, because the Messiah's true father is God. The implications of Jesus' question leaves the Pharisees speechless, and his question probably kept them up at night, because they expected a human Messiah, just as David was human, but Jesus' question makes the Pharisees wonder about their assumptions of a strictly human Messiah.

Jesus helps Pharisees to see a profound truth and they must have wondered, "Is it possible the Messiah will be superior even to King David our greatest king?"

64 Have I been so long with you, and *yet* you have not come to know Me, Philip?
John 14:9 (NASB)

"If you had known Me, you would have known My Father also; from now on you know Him, and have seen him." Philip said to Him, "Lord, show us the Father, and it is enough for us." Jesus said to him, "Have I been so long with you, and *yet* you have not come to know me Philip? He who has seen Me has seen the Father; how *can* you say, 'Show us the Father?' Do you not believe that I am in the Father, and the Father is in me? The words that I say to you I do not speak on my own initiative, but the Father abiding in Me does his works. Believe Me that I am in the Father and the Father is in Me; otherwise believe because of the works themselves."

John 14:7-11 (NASB)

Philip found it difficult to grasp the idea that Jesus is so close to God that to see Jesus was to see God. And yet, Jesus is not equal to the Father. Christians know some people distort Jesus' words to Philip to mean Jesus said he had equality with God. They are completely wrong; Jesus never said that. Remember his words in John:

"for the Father is greater than I."
John 14:28 (NASB)

For centuries some Jewish and Muslim religious leaders have taught that Christians think Jesus is a second god. Such teachings are untrue; but nevertheless, they teach this to disturb their followers and to discourage them from investigating Jesus and his teachings. Jesus made no assertion of equality with God, as we also read in Philippians.

> **Have this attitude in yourselves which was also in Christ Jesus, who, although He existed in the form of God, did not regard equality with God a thing to be grasped, but emptied Himself, taking the form of a bond-servant, and being made in the likeness of men.**
> **Philippians 2:5-7 (NASB)**

Some might argue, "Yes, but Jesus told Philip that to see him is to see God. Isn't that a contradiction? Isn't Jesus saying they look alike or are alike and if he says, and he did say, that seeing him is seeing God, isn't he saying they are equal?"

That's misreading the Bible and here's why: our human senses are wonderful but limited and it is only with insight that we go beyond our senses and perceive a reality greater than our senses are able to reveal to us. Most of us sense reality is not limited to what we can see and touch; we know there is a reality beyond our physical senses. Some people might say, "Well, maybe or maybe not. But since we cannot verify a reality beyond our senses, why bother to discuss it?" Here's why: the unseen reality is more important and more real than our physical reality; and the unseen reality is our ultimate destiny. Such a reality, or even the possibility of such a reality, is worth considering.

We are born to know the Truth. While the Enemy works to prevent us from learning the Truth, it exists nevertheless, and to deny the Truth is the same as denying God – because God is Truth. The conflict between Truth and lies will last until the end of time, and pretending there is no conflict is as nonsensical as pretending there is no light or darkness.

> **"for the Father is greater than I."**
> **John 14:28 (NASB)**

Regarding Jesus' statement that to see him is to see the Father, we need to remember that we think in physical terms with our limited senses; consequently, some might imagine Jesus means the Father looks like him physically with similar eyes, height, and weight, but that is childish thinking. Christians understand Jesus meant something else; they know these are great mysteries and they recall the beginning of John's Gospel.

> **In the beginning was the Word, and the Word was with God, and the Word was God. He was in the beginning with God.**
> **John 1:1-2 (NASB)**

One way to understand Jesus' declaration that to see him is to see the Father is to remember that God is light and to see the Messiah is to see that light.

Recall Jesus on the mountaintop with a few disciples who saw Jesus change in appearance, **"and His face shone like the sun, and His garments became as white as light."** (Matthew 17:2 NASB)

Remember Saul rushing to Damascus to arrest Christians.

> **As he was traveling, it happened that he was approaching Damascus, and suddenly a light**

from heaven flashed around him; and he fell to the ground and heard a voice saying to him, "Saul, Saul, why are you persecuting me?" And he said, "Who are you, Lord?"

And He *said*, "I am Jesus, whom you are persecuting, but get up and enter the city, and it will be told you what you must do."

Acts 9:3-6 (NASB)

Remember also Revelation 21:23 (NASB):

And the city has no need of the sun or of the moon to shine on it, for the glory of God has illumined it, and its lamp *is* the lamb.

And The First Letter of John:

God is light, and in Him there is no darkness at all.

1 John 1:5 (NASB)

And the Psalms:

In Your light we see light.

Psalm 36:9 (NASB)

Those following the teachings of Jesus follow the light.

Then Jesus again spoke to them, saying, "I am the Light of the world; he who follows Me will not walk in darkness, but will have the Light of life."

John 8:12 (NASB)

Now we see a little more clearly what Jesus meant when he said that to see him was to see the Father.

65 You fools and blind men! Which is more important, the gold or the temple that sanctified the gold?

Matthew 23:17 (NASB)

You foolish ones, did not He who made the outside make the inside also?

Luke 11:40 (NASB)

Woe to you, blind guides, who say, "Whoever swears by the temple, *that* is nothing; but whoever swears by the gold of the temple is obligated." You fools and blind men! Which is more important, the gold or the temple that sanctified the gold?

Matthew 23:16-17 (NASB)

Now when He had spoken, a Pharisee asked him to have lunch with him; and He went in, and reclined *at the table.* When the Pharisee saw it, he was surprised that He had not ceremonially washed before the meal. But the Lord said to him, "Now you Pharisees clean the outside of the cup and of the platter; but inside of you, you are full of robbery and wickedness. You foolish ones, did not He who made the outside make the inside also? But give that which is within as charity, and then all things are clean for you."

Luke 11:37-41 (NASB)

Both of these questions Jesus asks the Pharisees is really only about one thing – hierarchy. What is of greater value? What is holier? How do Pharisees with their years of religious training not understand this?

What is holier? The Lord's sanctuary or gold inside the sanctuary? What is more worthy? Ritual purity or spiritual purity? The outside or the inside of the cup? If it's inside, then let what is inside be given to charity and all is clean.

Again and again and yet again, Jesus brings his listener's attention to the importance of understanding God's Word. So when he asks the Pharisees which ranked higher, gold or the sanctuary, he reminds them of God's Word in Exodus:

> **You shall not make *other gods* besides Me; gods of silver or gods of gold, you shall not make for yourselves.**
>
> **Exodus 20:23 (NASB)**

The Messiah says to the Pharisees and to us that we must understand and respect hierarchy – we must know what ranks above something else and that the Creator of the Universe ranks above all.

> **66 And Jesus said to him, "Do you see these great buildings? Not one stone will be left upon another which will not be torn down,"**
>
> **Mark 13:2 (NASB)**

As He was going out of the temple, one of His disciples said to Him, "Teacher, behold what wonderful stones and what wonderful buildings!"

And Jesus said to him, "Do you see these great buildings? Not one stone will be left upon another which will not be torn down."

Mark 13:1-2 (NASB)

Jerusalem's Temple was world-famous, but when a disciple compliments its magnificence, Jesus ominously responds that the Temple was destined for destruction. The disciple must have been utterly shocked, because they probably assumed, as did many Jews at that time, that God would protect the Temple from harm – an assumption Rome's Legions would prove false 40 years later.

"Not one stone will be left upon another which will not be torn down."

A contrast: the Temple built by men is destroyed and remains in ruins 2,000 years later, but when men attempt to destroy God's Son he is raised up and lives. A Temple is brought down, but the Son of God is raised up. Jesus said this:

The Jews said to Him, "What sign do You show us as your authority for doing these things?" Jesus answered them, "Destroy this temple, and in three days I will raise it up."

John 2:18-19 (NASB)

Another contrast: men destroyed the Temple where God's presence had resided, but Christians will reside in God's presence in Heaven, where homes are prepared for them. Jesus said: **"In My Father's house are many dwelling places; if it were not so, I would have told you; for I go to prepare a place for you."**

John 14:2 (NASB)

> **67 Who then is the faithful and sensible slave whom his master put in charge of his household to give them their food at the proper time?**
>
> **Matthew 24:45 (NASB)**

Who then is the faithful and sensible slave who his master put in charge of his household to give them their food at the proper time? Blessed is that slave whom his master finds so doing when he comes.
Matthew 24:45-46 (NASB)

Jesus asks this question near the end of Matthew's 24th Chapter, a chapter that begins with the disciples asking him what signs would accompany his return and "the end of the age." Like a king counseling his troops before a battle, Jesus warns of the dangers his followers will face as the world blunders toward the tribulation.

What dangers does he mention? We can remember them by the five "D's" that the Devil brings as the age closes.

Deceptions: Phony messiahs will pull the wool over the eyes of many, and these fake messiahs will be joined by false prophets, who will mislead with their teachings and by miracles. "Then if anyone says to you, 'Behold here is the Christ,' or 'There *He is*,' do not believe *him*." (Matt 24:23 NASB). These deceivers will even try to fool God's chosen. Also, believe no one who gives precise predictions about the timing of the end, because no one knows the day or hour, not even the angels, not even the Son knows the day and hour, only God.

Disasters: Expect to read about massive crop failures causing food scarcity in some nations and large-scale regional famines.

Earthquakes – those widely feared convulsions – will increase in frequency. The damage earthquakes cause to property, and the disruptions they bring to travel by destroying bridges, roads, and airports will prevent the arrival of assistance to earthquake victims, and will hinder travel to family, friends, and work. Earthquakes can sweep massive ocean tides inland, such as the one in Indonesia that occurred the day after Christmas 2004, killing more than 200,000 people through a series of waves that flooded the coast. You might remember the earthquake in Japan of March 2011, the most powerful to ever hit Japan that triggered tidal waves – tsunamis –133 feet high. Loss of life was nearly 16,000, with another 3,600 missing. That 2011 Japanese quake was so powerful it shifted the earth's axis by several inches.

Death: There will be increasing talk, news and speculation about approaching wars. Jesus said nation will fight nation and kingdom will fight kingdom. **"When you hear of wars and rumors of wars, do not be frightened; *those things* must take place; but *that is* not yet the end." (Mark 13:7 NASB)**

Distress: Christians will be hated because they are loyal to Jesus of Nazareth, and they will be punished and some will be put to death. As the order of society breaks down, the love of some Christians will not endure, but Jesus promises Christians that those who endure to the end will be saved.

Desolation: Jesus warns about an "abomination of desolation" standing where it should not (Mark 13:14 NASB), no one should hesitate by trying to retrieve coats or goods from their homes, but they should immediately flee to the mountains.

These things are all birth-pangs of the new age. "This gospel of the kingdom shall be preached in the whole world as a testimony to all nations, and then the end will come."

(Matthew 24:14 NASB)

Jesus said no one knows the day of his return and that it will seem to be delayed. Yet, the Messiah will return at a time least expected.

> **Blessed is that slave whom his master finds so doing when he comes. Truly I say to you that he will put him in charge of all his possessions. But if that evil slave says in his heart, "My master is not coming for a long time, and begins to beat his fellow slaves and eat and drink with drunkards; the master of that slave will come on a day when he does not expect *him* and at an hour which he does not know, and will cut him in pieces and will assign him a place with the hypocrites; in that place there will be weeping and gnashing of teeth.**
> **Matthew 24:46-51 (NASB)**

> **He does not thank the slave because he did the things which are commanded, does he? So you too, when you do all the things which are commanded you, say, "We are unworthy slaves; we have done *only* that which we ought to have done."**
> **Luke 17:9-10 (NASB)**

Those who follow the Messiah accomplish their work in the world without boasting or self-praise or even notice, if they can help it, just as the Messiah did his work in Israel without drawing attention to himself.

68 "When did we see you ill or in prison, and come to visit you?"
Matthew 25:39

Then the king will say to those on his right, "You have my Father's blessing; come, take possession of the kingdom that has been ready for you since the world was made. For when I was hungry, you gave me food; when thirsty, you gave me drink; when I was a stranger, you took me into your home; when naked, you clothed me; when I was ill, you came to my help; when in prison, you visited me," Then the righteous will reply, **"Lord, when was it that we saw you hungry and fed you, or thirsty and gave you drink, a stranger and took you home, or naked and clothed you? When did we see you ill or in prison, and come to visit you?"** And the king will answer, "Truly I tell you: anything that you did for one of my brothers here, however insignificant, you did for me."

Matthew 25:34-40

Since the king has concealed himself in the hungry, the ill, and in prisoners, the understandably mystified person asked the king, "When did we see you ill or in prison?"

The Divine is hidden. We remember Mary could not recognize the resurrected Jesus, and at a later point in time after his resurrection, when Jesus was on the shores of the Galilee, his disciples didn't recognize him. And again, on the road to Emmaus, Jesus' friends did not recognize the resurrected Jesus even as he walked along side them and spoke to them. Divine Holiness is hidden from us, although some who are specially gifted can sometimes detect it.

Jesus' hidden Messiahship is a great mystery. **"He was in the world, and the world was made through Him, and the world did not know Him." (John 1:10 NASB)** John tells us the hidden Messiah can be found among the common. We do not know how Jesus is the prisoner or the sick. It may be that he is with them in love or in their humanness, or in spirit, or in all these ways and more, but we are aware that Jesus of Nazareth is with them in a way so true that anything we do for these people we are doing for him.

Mystery. For some, God is known yet unseen. For others, He is seen but unknown. He is known by those who believe in him, but remains unseen. Yet, for the agnostic and atheist, He is seen but unknown. Because He is evident by His creation, which the atheist sees and of which they are a part, and yet they reject what they see.

Paul explained God's hidden omnipresence to the Council of the Areopagus, saying, "though he is not far from each of us; for in Him we live and move and exist." (Acts 17:27-28 NASB)

Of special interest are the words, *"however insignificant."* **"Anything that you did for one of my brothers here, however insignificant, you did for me."** A promise that any assistance of any size is noted and recorded and will be rewarded.

Something else to consider: Matthew's passage, **"anything that you did for one of my brothers here … you did for me,"** is translated a bit differently in some versions of the Bible; it being translated either as **"one of my brothers,"** or **"one of these least brothers of mine,"** **(New American Bible),** or **"one of the least of these brothers of mine," (Matthew 25:40, New Jerusalem Bible)** or **"one of the least who are members of my family." (NRSV).** We remember earlier in Matthew (12:50) Jesus identified his brother, sister, and mother as "Whoever does the will of my Heavenly Father." Should we conclude then that only assistance to fellow Christians (who Jesus called his true brothers, sisters, and mother) is what will be rewarded?

Jesus seems to say helping a *follower* of Jesus is helping Jesus himself, yet Jesus also taught to help everyone, including *enemies.* Serious thinking is required here. This is something Christians should contemplate in conversations with other Christians and in Bible study groups. Those will be interesting conservations.

What inspired Jesus to teach visiting the ill, the imprisoned, clothing the naked, and giving food to the hungry and drink to the thirsty? The inspiration was Jesus' authoritative knowledge of Torah and the prophets. Notice how close Jesus' words (in Matthew 25:34-40) are to Ezekiel:

> **Consider the man who is righteous and does what is just and right. ... he oppresses no one, he return's the debtor's pledge, he never commits robbery; he gives his food to the hungry and clothes to those who have none. ... Such a one is righteous: he will live, says the Lord God.**
>
> **Ezekiel 18:5,7-9**

And see Jesus echoing Isaiah:

> **Is that what you call a fast, a day acceptable to the Lord? Rather, is this not the fast that I require: to loose the fetters of injustice, to untie the knots of the yoke, and set free those who are oppressed, tearing off every yoke?**
>
> **Is it not sharing your food with the hungry, taking the homeless poor into your house, clothing the naked when you meet them, and never evading a duty to your kinsfolk?**
>
> **Isaiah 58:5-7**

Jesus teaches the prophetic word.

69 Why do you bother the woman? For she has done a good deed to Me.
Matthew 26:10 (NASB)

> **But Jesus, aware of this, said to them, "Why do you bother the woman? For she has done a good deed to Me. For you always have the poor with you; but you do not always have Me. For when she poured this perfume on My body, she did it to prepare Me for burial. Truly I say to you, wherever this gospel is preached in the whole world, what this woman has done will also be spoken of in memory of her."**
> **Matthew 26:10-13 (NASB)**

The disciples resented her pouring perfume over Jesus' head because they knew many poor people could have been helped with the money it cost to buy the expensive perfume. While the disciples saw a lost opportunity to help the poor, Jesus saw an exceptional moment in time.

In this case, the disciples did not grasp that the woman's gift transcended its price. Questions about the use of money are with us today as some people see the money spent on royal weddings, or security protection for dignitaries, or for the construction of churches, and they think it be better if that money were given to the poor instead. Jesus said the poor will always be among you – that financial inequality will always be a fact. Christians understand that while this is true, it is no excuse to ignore the poor; but Christians also know that right relations with the Almighty are more important than economic philosophy or efforts to redistribute resources "fairly," a word understood differently at different times by different people. Christians also know right conduct toward the poor is part of right relations with the God. They know the God of Israel is a God of justice who requires justice for all who work and for all who want to work but cannot. The God of justice wants justice done for those with property as well as for those without. The God of Israel does not want enmity between those with much and those with little.

Beyond considerations of rich or poor, there is something else in Matthew 26 that is alien to our 21st century thinking – which are, omens. Many view omens as belonging to the superstitious past. Jesus, however, sees an omen in the woman's act, a portent of his burial, a foreshadowing that he would soon die and be buried. (As you know, after Jesus died, women from Galilee watched where his body was placed, then went home and prepared spices and perfumes, waiting for the Sabbath to end so they go to his tomb and bring the spices and perfumes. See Luke 23:55-56)

Jesus knew the religious elites would sentence him to death and he knew also the woman, although she was not aware of it, was preparing him for death. She is still remembered for her generous heart. It seemed neither she nor the disciples saw the shrouded meaning of her perfume, Jesus told them, but they probably thought he was speaking symbolically.

> **70 And Jesus asked him, "What is your name?"**
>
> **Luke 8:30 (NASB)**

And Jesus asked him, "What is your name?" And he said, "Legion"; for many demons had entered him. They were imploring Him not to command them to go away into the abyss.

Luke 8:30-31 (NASB)

Jesus and his men had just sailed across the Sea of Galilee and when they disembarked from their boat, a madman charged directly toward them, then dropped to the ground in front of Jesus and screamed,

145

"What business do we have with each other, Jesus, Son of the Most High God? I beg You, do not torment me." (Luke 8:28 NASB) Jesus had been ordering the unclean spirit to leave the man.

The locals knew this man. He went naked and bashed himself with rocks until he bled. He howled night and day and lived among the tombs. No one would use the road that passed near him. Some had tried to restrain him with chains, but he always broke free. He was chained to the devil.

> **And Jesus asked him, "What is your name?" And he said, "Legion"**
> (There are parallel reports in **Matthew 8:28-34 / Mark 5:9 / Luke 8:30**)

Why would the Messiah ask the possessed man his name? Why would he bother? There are Biblically well-established reasons why Jesus would ask the man his name.

Names are exceptionally important in the Old and New Testaments. Remember that an angel told Joseph his wife Mary would bear a son and the child was to be named Jesus. Remember the angel Gabriel told Zechariah his prayers had been heard and his wife would bear him a son who was to be named "John." Remember also Jesus renamed Simon as Peter, which as you know means "the Rock". While both Jesus and John (in Hebrew: Yeshua and Yochanon) were common names in those times, it seems God does not trust human judgment to choose the right names for those He has especially destined for divine tasks.

Not only do names have certain properties in the Bible, but also knowing a person's name grants a kind of capability to the person who knows the name. Even today, when a Roman Catholic priest performs an exorcism through the power of God, the priest asks the name of the spirit or spirits that possess the individual.

This encounter with the possessed man shows Jesus was both human and divine. The demons possessing the man recognize Jesus as the Son of God – even at a distance – and they know Jesus has the power to punish them. So the demons plead with the Messiah, "Have you come here to torment us before the time?" (Matthew 8:29 NASB) (They know Jesus will judge all at the End of Time.) But it seems Jesus does not know their names. Does this show that his knowledge, at least at that time and place, was human? I think this event tells us Jesus had both divine power from his Father, and human knowledge requiring that he ask the name of the spirits who possessed the man. As a man, Jesus had human knowledge, but as the Son of God, he displayed wisdom and knowledge no human could have.

71 Who touched my clothes?

Mark 5:30

Who touched my clothes? Mark 5:30

Who is the one who touched Me? Luke 8:45 (NASB)

Crowds press in on Jesus with so many people that he can hardly breathe. In the crowd is a determined woman, who squeezes through the crowd, pushing past one person, then another, and another until she finally reaches the rabbi's back, where I imagine she makes a final, frantic leap to reach Jesus, arm extended, she falls to the ground, face in the dust, but manages to touch the tassel of the rabbi's cloak. The bleeding from her 12-year hemorrhage stops. At that instant Jesus knew someone was healed. "Who touched my clothes," he said, to which his disciples reply, "You see the crowd pressing around you and yet you ask, 'Who touched me?'" "But he kept looking around to see who had done it." (Mark 5:30-32)

The healed woman knew Jesus knew someone had touched his clothing and so goes to him. She was trembling, fearful and fell down at his feet and told him the truth, and explained that she had heard of him and told herself that if she could only touch his clothes, she would be healed. Doctors could not cure her, even though she had spent all her money on them. Jesus listened and said, "Daughter, your faith has healed you. Go in peace, free from your affliction." (Mark 5:34)

Were there others in the crowd who wanted to be healed of their sickness, touched Jesus, but were not healed because they lacked the woman's faith? We don't know. We do know this woman touched the cloak of Jesus and was healed, and we also know that she had faith that she would be healed.

Like the previous miracle story, we once again notice Jesus' divine power and yet his limited human knowledge. The Son of God through his Father's power had healed a person and yet Jesus asks whom it was that he had healed.

Two points in the story remind us of Jesus' Jewishness. The first is the woman touching the fringe on Jesus' cloak (one translation calls it the "tassel" of his cloak). Jesus was probably wearing a tallit, a prayer garment described in the Book of Numbers, the fourth book of the Bible, where the Lord says to the Israelites: Make tassels on the corners of your garments. The tassel was to have a violet thread woven into it, and whenever the Israelites saw the tassel, it was to serve as a token reminder to keep themselves holy, and to remain consecrated to the God. It is likely this was the tallit/fringe on Jesus' cloak that the woman had touched.

(See Numbers 15:37-40 and Deuteronomy 22:12)

The second aspect of this story regarding Jesus' Jewishness concerns this woman's hemorrhage, which the Torah says (see Leviticus 15:25-31) would have made her impure, and moreover, she could have transmitted her impurity to others, even through contact with an intermediate, inanimate object, such as a chair. So the woman who touched Jesus' fringe was unclean and in that condition, according to the Law, touching the clothing of Jesus' would have outraged the priests. For these reasons, we can imagine the woman's fear when Jesus discovered she had touched him. She probably thought that she had offended this holy man by touching him in her unclean status – and she may have been very worried about what he might say to her. Yet, what the Law considered impure was returned to health when the impure person had approached Jesus in faith.

Jesus taught a form of purity more important than ritual purity. We saw this when a Pharisee invited Jesus to dinner; Jesus accepted, sat down and prepared to eat without washing his hands at the Pharisee's home, who was surprised and offended.

> **But the Lord said to him, "Now you Pharisees clean the outside of the cup and of the platter; but inside of you, you are full of robbery and wickedness. You foolish ones, did not He who made the outside make the inside also?"**
>
> **Luke 11:39-40 (NASB)**

The woman with a 12-year hemorrhage was made clean. Was the observant Pharisee made clean by washing his hands?

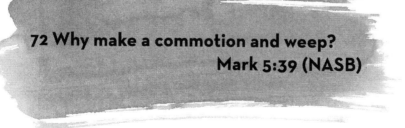

72 Why make a commotion and weep?
Mark 5:39 (NASB)

And entering in, He said to them, "Why make a commotion and weep? The child has not died, but is asleep."

Mark 5:39-40 (NASB)

Synagogue leader Jairus' 12-year-old girl is at death's door and he pleads with Jesus to lay his hands on her and save her. As Jesus heads to Jairus' home a messenger arrives and says the little girl has died and the Master shouldn't be troubled any further. But Jesus tells Jairus, **"Do not be afraid *any longer*, only believe."** (Mark 5:36 NASB)

From his 12 disciples, Jesus chooses three – Peter, John, and James – and the girl's mother and father. As Jesus and his group of five arrive at Jairus' home, they hear loud wailing for the dead girl. Then Jesus asks what seems to us an odd and almost nonsensical question: **"Why make a commotion and weep? The child has not died, but is asleep."** One gospel says flute-players were among the mourners, suggesting they were professional mourners; and, if they are, they would have been annoyed to hear Jesus tell them the little girl was only sleeping, because as professional mourners they knew a corpse when they saw one; and, moreover, if Jesus was right and the girl was only sleeping, they would lose their fees for singing lamentations. But this is a side issue and we won't let it distract us from the more important issue of faith.

Jesus sends all the other people out of the house and takes his group of five to the room where the dead girl lie. Taking the dead girl's hand, Jesus says, "Get up, my child," and life returns to her. Jesus tells the astonished group in the room to give her something to eat and also tells them not to say a word to anyone outside what they have just seen – a dead girl returning to life.

Perhaps we now see why Jesus told the mourners the girl was only sleeping – he did not want them to know he had performed a miracle – *better to let them think she was only* sleeping. Note also Judas was not a part of the group of five who witnessed this miracle, nor was Thomas. Judas would betray Jesus and Thomas would doubt Jesus' resurrection. Would Judas and Thomas have acted differently had they witnessed this miracle of the power of life over death? Or were Judas and Thomas not invited to be part of the group of five because they lacked the faith of Peter, John and James?

I was once on the staff of a man who worked himself and his whole staff at an adrenalized rate. He had a good mind and was interesting to talk with on any topic, and although Jewish, he greatly enjoyed the spirit of the Christmas holidays and generously gave his staff wonderful Christmas gifts. He was also witty. Once, as we talked about religion, I remember him observing, partly in jest, "Well, dead people don't come back to life – at least in my religion, they don't."

If you have had a few jobs, you have no doubt learned the boss is always right. Even if you are certain they are wrong, it is unwise to tell them or even think it, lest they sense dissent in your attitude. So I did not contradict my boss when he said, "dead people don't come back to life – at least in my religion, they don't," and I accepted that, as a Jew, he meant the idea of Jesus returning to life was nonsense, and he probably would have thought the same about Lazarus or Jairus' little girl.

Someone bolder might have told my boss that people have indeed risen from the dead in Judaism, and, in fact, did so in cases very similar to Jairus' daughter. The Jewish Bible records when the Prophet Elijah was a house guest of a widow in Zarephath, and the widow's son died, Elijah called out to God, "O Lord, my God, I pray You, let this child's life return to him." And the Lord heard Elijah's prayer and the child returned to life.

(1 Kings 17:21 NASB)

Second Kings records a similar story about Elijah's successor, Elisha. When Elisha travelled by the home of a certain a wealthy couple, he would stop there because they were kind toward him, and had arranged a small accommodation for the holy man with a bed, table, seat, and lamp. One day when the couple's son became ill and died, the woman sought Elisha's help. Responding to the woman's request, Elisha and his assistant went to her home, where she had put her son's body on Elisha's guest bed. Elisha shut the door, and except for his assistant, Elisha was alone with the boy's body. Elisha prayed to the Lord and the boy's eyes opened. His mother was called, and the Prophet Elisha said to her, "Take up your son."

(2 Kings 4:36 NASB)

And yet another Old Testament report of a dead person returning to life: as a burial party was bringing a deceased man to his grave, they saw bandits approaching, so the burial party panicked, and threw the body into the Prophet Elisha's grave. When the dead man's body touched the prophet's bones he returned to life.

(See 2 Kings 13:21)

So we see the God of Israel did indeed raise the dead prior to Lazarus and Jesus. So if a Jewish person tells you that their religion cannot accept a person returning from the dead, you may politely point out that the idea of the dead returning to life is a very Jewish concept and it can be found in the Jewish Bible (or Old Testament as Christians generally refer to it). The Elijah and Elisha stories are in the ninth book of Jewish Bible, in Melakim (which means "Kings"), and in the section of the Jewish Bible called Nebi'im – Prophets. But if the Jewish individual in question happens to be your boss, may the Holy Spirit guide your words and Jesus protect your job.

73 Why does this generation seek for a sign?

Mark 8:12 (NASB)

The Pharisees came out and began to argue with Him, seeking from Him a sign from heaven, to test Him. Sighing deeply in His spirit, He said, "Why does this generation seek for a sign? Truly I say to you, no sign will be given to this generation." Leaving them, He again embarked and went to the other side.

Mark 8:11-13 (NASB)

There are two interesting questions about Mark 8:11:

Why *did* Pharisees need a sign? And why *didn't* Jesus perform one?

The first question – *Why did Pharisees need a sign?* – concerns wanting proof. Jews sought proof because they remembered Moses showed signs to the Pharaoh, who finally accepted Egypt's plagues and pestilences were from God. Thus, Jewish religious leaders wanted a sign as proof Jesus' power was from God, but in asking for that proof, they, like Pharaoh, were challenging God.

Second question – *Why didn't Jesus give the Pharisees a sign?* – concerns who is teaching whom. Who needs to pass the test, the teacher or the student? The student, of course, and Pharisees were the students – the Pharisees just didn't know it. It is the Pharisees' understanding of the Law, Moses, and the Prophets that is being tested.

So then, *why didn't Jesus give them a sign so they would accept him as Messiah?* Jewish leaders seemed to say, "Perform a miracle and we'll believe you are the Messiah!" After all, Jesus had performed many miracles, so why not perform one more for Jewish religious and political leaders?

But notice a recurring feature of Jesus' miracles:

When Jesus cured a man of leprosy, he told the man not to tell anyone.
(See Luke 5:14)

When Jesus brought Jairus' daughter back to life, he gave Jairus and his wife strict instructions not to let anyone know.
(See Mark 5:43)

At Bethsaida, Jesus cured a blind man, but after this miracle, he told him not to even go into the village, because it appears Jesus did not want any news of the miracle to travel by word of mouth.
(See Mark 8:26)

When Jesus changed water to wine at the Cana wedding, the wedding guests were unaware.
(See John 2:9)

When two blind men followed Jesus and begged him for pity, Jesus restored their sight and told them sternly, "See that no one hears about this."
(See Matthew 9:27-31)

When Pilate sent Jesus to Herod Antipas, Herod was excited because he had heard of Jesus' miracles and hoped to see one, but when Herod questioned Jesus, Jesus did not answer Herod or provide a sign.
(See Luke 23:6-9)

Jesus of Nazareth did not produce miracles for public entertainment, but for people in need and usually in a private setting. When Jesus fasted in the wilderness, the Enemy tempted him to use his God-given powers for his own benefit, but Jesus would not.

(See Matthew 4:3-10)

Jesus knew the Pharisees *had witnessed* miracles, but they denounced the miracles and accused him of working through the devil.

> **And when the demon had been cast out, the one who had been mute spoke, and the crowds were amazed and said, "Never has anything like this been seen in Israel." But the Pharisees said, "By the ruler of the demons he casts out demons."**
> **Matthew 9:32-34 (New Revised Standard Version)**

Jesus quoted Isaiah to the disbelieving Pharisees: "You will keep on hearing, but will not understand; You will keep on seeing but will not perceive."

(Matthew 13:14 NASB)

Understand something: one of Jesus' greatest miracles to raise Lazarus from the dead – but even that did not persuade the religious leaders. Instead, when they heard about Lazarus the chief priests and Pharisees "convened a council" and "from that day on they planned together to kill" Jesus.

(See John 11:47 and 53 NASB)

Does faith come from miracles or from hearing God's Word? You know the story Jesus told of a wealthy man who wore the best clothes and had the best food, while the poor man outside his gates dreamed of having scrapes from the rich man's table. The poor man was named Lazarus and when he died the angels carried him off to heaven. The rich man died and was buried, judged, and went to Hades. From Hades, the rich man called out to Abraham in heaven and begged Abraham to send the poor man to his five brothers to warn them so "they may not come to this place of torment." But Abraham told him, "They have Moses and the prophets; let them listen to them." The rich man replied that if someone came back from the dead, they would listen and repent, but Abraham answered, "If they do not listen to Moses and the prophets they will pay no heed even if someone should rise from the dead."

Luke 16:28-31

The parable is clear: God's Word is reason enough to believe. Here is something else to consider: a need for miracles can actually blind people to the truth. There is a miracle worker who is coming… the world knows him by one name, but Christians know him by another: it is the Antichrist and when the Antichrist comes he will perform miracles to deceive Christians and undermine their faith. He will fail to deceive true Christians, even though millions will be deceived and follow him to Armageddon and Hades.

> **It worked great miracles, even making fire come down from heaven to earth, where people could see it. By the miracles it was allowed to perform in the presence of the beast it deluded the inhabitants of earth, and persuaded them to erect an image in honour of the beast which had been wounded by the sword and yet lived.**
>
> **Revelation 13:13-14**

Nonbelievers who insist on miracles will have them, but followers of the Messiah do not need miracles.

If we understand Jesus' question, **"Why does this generation seek a sign? Truly I say to you, no sign will be given to this generation."** we will recognize an important Biblical truth: the Kingdom of Heaven is invisible to the world, and another truth – Holiness often hides, while evil seeks fame, acclaim, and flattery. Evil is arrogant. This truth helps Christians know before others who is evil: because the Christian always suspects the person receiving the highest praise, the loudest applause, and the most prestigious awards. Christians know such a person is under suspicion, because they remember the Master's warning:

> *Woe to you* **when all men speak well of you, for their fathers used to treat the false prophets in the same way.**
>
> **(Luke 6:26 NASB)**

This is not only a warning about how to recognize false prophets and false Christians, but how to identify the Antichrist – whom many in the world are now preparing to worship and follow – they just don't know it yet.

But not all will worship the beast, the Antichrist. The Book of Revelation says everyone will worship the beast, except those whose names are in the book of life of the Lamb. (See Revelation 13:8)

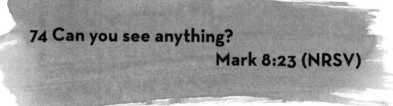

74 Can you see anything?
Mark 8:23 (NRSV)

They came to Bethsaida. Some people brought a blind man to him and begged him to touch him. He took the blind man by the hand and led him out of the village; and when he had put saliva on his eyes and laid his hands on him, he asked him, "Can you see anything?" And the man looked up and said, "I can see people, but they look like trees, walking." Then Jesus laid his hands on his eyes again; and he looked intently and his sight

was restored, and he saw everything clearly. Then he sent him away to his home, saying, "Do not even go into the village."
Mark 8:22-26 (New Revised Standard Version)

Even holy men and women find the power of God mysterious. Remember the Prophet Elisha was a friend of a woman whose son died unexpectedly? When the woman sought Elisha's help, Elisha did not respond himself, but instead gave his staff to his assistant Gehazi, telling him to put the staff on the dead boy and he would return to life. Gehazi followed instructions, but the boy remained dead. The mother had never left Elisha's side, perhaps suspecting the prophet himself would be needed to return her son to life. Hearing that his staff had not brought the boy back to life, Elisha went to the woman's house, entered the room and shut the door to the room where the dead boy lay and prayed to the God of Israel, then Elisha embraced the boy, the Bible says, "his eyes to his eyes, and his hands to his hands," (2 Kings 4:34) and the child's body became warm, but still this was not enough to bring the boy back to life, Elisha had to repeat the ritual seven times before the boy came back to life.

Contrast this miracle with Jesus curing the Centurion's servant – where only Jesus' word was needed to cure the servant at a distance. And then contrast curing the Centurion's servant with Jesus spitting on the blind man's eyes, laying his hands on him, and asking if he could see; the blind man said he could not see very well, so Jesus laid hands on him again, and then the man saw clearly.

There is a message for us regarding the mystery of God's power. Prayers are not magic, and sometimes even the holiest of individuals may need a first, second, third, or fourth attempt to effect healing. So followers of the Messiah's do not despair when their prayers are not immediately answered in a way they expect – they are Holy communications with God and God hears.

We remember Jesus' story about an unjust judge with no respect for men or fear of God, yet a widow wouldn't give up and relentlessly pestered the judge for legal protection from her opponent. The unjust judge realized if he didn't grant the widow justice, she would never stop hounding him. Jesus said if that was how an unjust judge acted, who at last granted the widow's request, then think how quickly a just God responds to those who ask for help. (See Luke 18:1-7)

75 What were you discussing on the way?
Mark 9:33 (NASB)

> **They came to Capernaum; and when He was in the house, He *began* to question them, "What were you discussing on the way?" But they keep silent, for on the way they had discussed with one another which *of them was* the greatest.**
> **Mark 9:33-34 (NASB)**

New York Times columnist David Brooks wrote of "Machiavellians in politics," describing some of them as, "nakedly ambitious people who are always strategizing, sometimes ruthlessly, for their own personal advantage." Brooks said other types of these Machiavellians feign "affection for those who might be useful."[7]

Having worked inside Washington's Beltway for many years, I was frequently impressed by how carefully some people calculated career advancement, they obsessively sought friendships with the

---

[7] The New York Times, David Brooks, December 11, 2015, A 41

influential, elbowed competitors out of their path and brooded over any setback. That attitude is not new to Washington – even the apostles seemed to have some of it.

Many professional people are disquieted to hear Jesus say: **"If anyone wants to be first, he shall be last of all and servant of all."** (Mark 9:35 NASB) This seems directly contrary to our daily lives and our instincts and shows how far our thinking is from God's. "For My thoughts are not your thoughts, Nor are your ways My ways." declares the Lord. (Isaiah 55:8 NASB)

Remember that even Peter failed to understand God's will for the Messiah, causing Jesus to rebuke Peter:

"Get behind Me, Satan! You are a stumbling block to Me; for you are not setting your mind on God's interests, but man's." (Matthew 16:23 NASB)

While we look out for Number One, the Messiah says to place ourselves last. We don't want to think about this, because we live in an upside-down world after The Fall. The Messiah teaches us how to place our lives in the right order.

> **"If anyone wants to be first, he shall be last of all and servant of all."**
>
> **Mark 9:35 (NASB)**

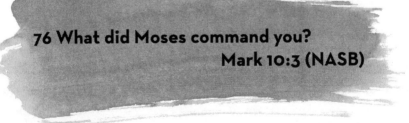

76 What did Moses command you?
Mark 10:3 (NASB)

> *Some* **Pharisees came up to Jesus, testing Him, and**
> ***began* to question Him whether it was lawful for a**
> **man to divorce a wife. And He answered and said**
> **to them, "What did Moses command you?" They**
> **said, "Moses permitted *a man* to write a certificate**
> **of divorce and send her away." But Jesus said to**
> **them, "Because of your hardness of heart he wrote**
> **you this commandment. But from the beginning**
> **of creation, God made them male and female. For**
> **this reason a man shall leave his father and mother,**
> **and the two shall become one flesh. What therefore**
> **God has joined together, let no man separate."**
>
> **Mark 10:2-9 (NASB)**

We can assume the wisdom of divorce was in doubt during Jesus' lifetime; otherwise, they would not have asked this question, which Jesus answers with a question of his own, "What did Moses command you?" Moses only requires paperwork, they replied, just a certificate for a man to divorce a woman. Right, Jesus says, but Moses was making an accommodation to your hard hearts – a compromise to God's original intention. God intended a faithful and lasting bond until death.

While the issue of divorce is important, there is something else going on here that would have enraged the Pharisees more than Jesus' teaching on divorce. Can you guess what it would have been?

If you cannot, imagine you're a Pharisee, a highly educated religious leader. As a Pharisee, you spent years studying Torah and the Law. You have participated in countless discussions about the Law with wise men. You move among an influential class of people and you have their respect. These people consider you a righteous Jew who keeps, protects, and interprets the Law. So what did Jesus say that angers you?

You are angry because Jesus claims he knows *why* Moses pronounced divorce permissible. Jesus is also saying he *knows God's original plan,* in effect saying he is more knowledgeable about the Law than you and other Pharisees, and Jesus is claiming to return the Law to its original purpose. One more thing, Jesus is also saying that divorce was only permitted only because of their hard hearts, aiming his critical comment, it seems, at Pharisees, at least in part. This is not something the Pharisees want to hear, and any Jew saying such things is dangerous to Pharisees, priests, Sadducees, scribes, and the entire religious establishment.

The argument is becoming who really understands Moses and the Law. Is it the respected Jewish leadership or a Jew from Nazareth with no connections and an unknown education? If you were a Pharisee and had heard what Jesus taught about divorce, what would you think?

77 Is it not written, "My house shall be called a house of prayer for all the nations?"

Mark 11:17 (NASB)

Then they came to Jerusalem. And He entered the temple and began to drive out those who were buying and selling in the temple, and overturned the tables of the money changers and the seats of those who were selling doves; and He would not permit anyone to carry merchandise through the temple. And He *began* to teach and to say to them, "Is it not written, 'My house shall be called a house of prayer for all the nations'? But you have made it a robbers' den."

Mark 11:15-17 (NASB)

When Jesus saw business being conducted at the Temple, he did not think it was time for a discussion or time to seek a compromise solution. He acted and thrashed the Temple merchants with a whip, scattered their money, and pushed them and the animals they were selling out of the temple. Shocked religious leaders wanted to know his authority for this action. Who did this Jesus of Nazareth think he was?

Imagine how our political and religious experts might interpret Jesus' actions if they happened today?

What would Conservatives say today about Jesus and the Temple?

The Conservatives would say Jesus has no respect for capitalism or private property. They would say the sale of sacrificial animals has been going on for years and benefits not only sellers, but the buyers; moreover, it benefits the temple itself, and, thus, the Law of Moses, which instituted temple worship. So Conservatives would say, this Leftist, anti-capitalist Jesus rages onto the scene, interrupts peaceful, lawful selling of goods, which the people clearly want and need for worship. Even the high priest and rabbis have purchased sacrificial animals at the temple! And by the way, today's Conservatives might add: what are the thousands of pilgrims supposed to do when they visit the Temple? They need the correct coins, so, we have professional moneychangers conveniently on-hand at the Temple to provide that service. Should we expect pilgrims to tramp all over Jerusalem hunting for moneychangers when we can provide the service right here at the Temple?

The moneychangers offer some payments to temple officials for their space in the Temple's Court of the

Gentiles, and that is only fair; after all, it's valuable property! Jesus doesn't understand business; he doesn't understand how the world works, he doesn't understand how friends help each other to make money to their mutual benefit. So temple business offends Jesus! Well what of the thousands of others who are not offended by it? What about them! Jesus needs to understand how the free flow of goods and money benefits everyone. Jesus understands nothing of how the world works and his actions prove it!

What would Progressives say today about Jesus and the Temple?

Progressives would say the man from Nazareth did not study at the right religious schools and he associates with the petty bourgeois classes, and consequently holds reactionary religious views, with an emphasis on conservative prophetic thinking. Progressives would think his attack on the moneychangers showed evidence of a rising anti-capitalist consciousness, but he was only nibbling around the edges of true revolutionary change against the oppressive power structures of the old Jewish Guard and Roman Imperialism. Moreover, Jesus is confused. He is supposedly a "Man of Peace," but he violently attacks petty capitalist moneychangers, while he forbids the sale of cattle, sheep, and doves, and even bans them from the Temple mount. We know the rich can buy oxen, and the middle class can buy sheep for sacrifices, but what about the poor? Doves are the only sacrifice the poor can afford! Jesus likes to teach about the poor, but if he were really concerned about them, why wouldn't he at least permit the sale of the doves to the poor? How politically unaware Jesus is! How ignorant of the underlying economic laws governing all history. Sure, he threw out the capitalist moneychangers and their money – but if he really cared about the poor, he would have gathered up their money and given it to the poor. Or at least, he should have used that money to subsidize the purchase of doves for the poor. As it is, all that Jesus really did was irritate the capitalist power structure with no lasting effect on the oppressed. Jesus understands nothing of how the world works and his actions prove it!

What would Moderates say today about Jesus and the Temple?

Those in the middle, the moderates seeking compromise solutions would say Jesus should have shown more restraint regarding sales of sacrificial animals on the temple mount before expelling the moneychangers. Shouldn't Jesus have sought a middle ground in this disagreement to avoid violence? Why did he feel it was necessary to overturn the tables of small businessmen? Why the violence?

It seems Jesus of Nazareth wanted a fight! Oh dear, how uncompromising is this man and how extreme! Why didn't he reason with the moneychangers? Perhaps persuade them to restrict their business hours to three hours each day, or maybe fewer days a week – five days instead of six? Jesus is divisive! Does he deliberately seek to upset the most intelligent and influential men of Israel? Yes, he teaches, "Love your enemies," but then he whips unarmed businessmen! I tell you, this is why we moderates seek the regulation of whips, in the hands of the self-righteous, they can be dangerous weapons. A so-called "Man of Peace"? Indeed! Yet he attacks tax-paying merchants who only seek to provide for their families. Now we hear

JONAH BEN-JOSEPH

wild talk from some that he is the Messiah! If that idea becomes widely accepted, we can expect more extremism and trouble. His unreasonable actions on the temple mount show us that this Jesus of Nazareth understands nothing about how the world works and his actions prove it!

Whether in 33AD or today, people who reject Jesus will find reasons to do so – whether their reasons are political, philosophical, economic, scientific or religious. If you view Jesus through one of these lenses, you will not understand him. Politics and philosophy are worthwhile, but Jesus is beyond them. He is the Son of God.

Jesus' actions against the Temple merchants show how interwoven his life was with prophecy, when he said, **"Is it not written, 'My house shall be called a house of prayer for all the nations'?"** Jesus was referencing Isaiah (56:7 NASB):

> "For My house will be called a house of prayer for all the peoples."

And by calling it a "bandits' cave" he was quoting Jeremiah:

> "Has this house, which is called by My name, become a den of robbers in your sight? Behold I, even I, have seen *it*." declares the Lord.
>
> (Jeremiah 7:11 NASB)

By putting an end to the money changing and sales of sacrificial animals, Jesus makes Zechariah's prophecy reality:

> "And there shall no longer be traders in the house of the Lord of hosts on that day."
>
> (Zechariah 14:21 NRSV)

166

When Jesus drives out the temple merchants, he fulfills the prophecy of Hosea:

"I will drive them out of my house!"

(Hosea 9:15 NASB)

Jesus of Nazareth appeared extreme to the experts of his day. What would today's world think of him? What would people think if they saw a video of Jesus of Nazareth driving the merchants out of the Temple? How would today's media report it? Would the internet reports today be favorable to Jesus or to those he pushed out of the Temple?

78 Which of these three do you think proved to be a neighbor to the man who fell into the robbers' hands?
Luke 10:36 (NASB)

Which of these three do you think proved to be a neighbor to the man who fell into the robbers' hands? And he said, "The one who showed mercy toward him." Then Jesus said to him, "Go and do the same."

Luke 10:36-37 (NASB)

As Jesus was teaching about concern for your neighbor, a lawyer asked, "But who is my neighbor?" wanting a definition of "neighbor." Jesus answered with a parable about a big-hearted Samaritan, but the story is not as simple as it first appears.

It concerns a man travelling from Jerusalem to Jericho, telling us he "went down" from Jerusalem. I have travelled the Jerusalem-Jericho road. It is a desolate, desert road descending lower and lower until it reaches Jericho, which is one of the lowest elevations on earth.

On his way to Jericho, a man was robbed and beaten and left in the dirt road. Potential help arrives when a priest comes on the scene, but he does not help, and instead he passes by on the opposite side of the road. A Levite later comes along, sees the wounded man, but he also passes by on the other side of the road. One reason both priest and Levite may have passed by the victim could have been their concerns over purity; because if the man were actually dead, touching him would have made them ritually impure, so they may have valued their purity more than they valued a stranger.

A passing Samaritan reacted positively to the wounded man, picked him up, brought him to an inn, and made sure the man received all the care he needed.

We can see the lawyer asked Jesus the wrong question. The question is not, "Who is my neighbor?" but rather *who will be the neighbor* to the man needing help?

As lawyers are trained to do, the lawyer wanted definitions and legal limits to his responsibility – but Jesus says be like the Samaritan who saw a chance to do good. Note something else (frequently stated, but worth repeating): Priests and Levites were highly respected and viewed as experts in the Law, while Samaritans were considered by Jews to be a mixed race people who rejected the full scope of the Jewish Law. Yet, it was the Samaritan with limited knowledge of the Law who fulfilled the Law.

With hostile relations between Samaritans and Jews, a parable featuring a Samaritan as the hero would have disquieted Jewish sensibilities. But Jesus not only unsettled Jewish thinking about Samaritans, he also challenged Samaritan thinking about Jews. To understand, we need a little background on Jewish-Samaritan relations.

For Jews, the word *"Samaritan"* was a negative term and was used as an insult. Remember Jews had attacked Jesus by saying to him, "Do we not say rightly that You are a Samaritan and have a demon?"

(John 8:48 NASB)

Both Samaritans and Jews viewed themselves as the real Jews. Samaritans thought they were the authentic Jews because they followed the Law of Moses and rejected the later additions to the Bible. Meanwhile, Jews thought the Samaritans were racial half-breeds, descendents of Arab peoples who had intermarried with Jews, and also thought that the Samaritans only practiced a lesser form of basic Judaism.

Jewish-Samaritan relations were cold. Remember the messengers who were sent ahead to a Samaritan town to prepare a reception for Jesus, but the Samaritans were unwelcoming. That rudeness so outraged James and John that they requested permission from Jesus to "command fire to come down from heaven and consume" the Samaritan town. (James and John's request makes us wonder: had they seen Jesus do something similar before? Otherwise, why would they have thought of "fire from heaven"?) Jesus rebuked the two apostle's request, and instead Jesus did what evangelists do even today when they encounter an unfriendly reception – they went to a different town. (see Luke 9:54)

Jews and Samaritans also disagreed on sacrifice; Samaritans said sacrifices should be offered on Samaria's Mount Gerizim, while Jews believed sacrifices should be at Jerusalem's Temple. Jesus spoke to the Samaritan woman at the well and told her that such disputes over the places to sacrifice should become a thing of the past, and tells the woman what kind of worship the God of Israel wants.

"Believe me," said Jesus, "the time is coming when you will worship the Father neither on this mountain nor in Jerusalem. You Samaritans

worship you know not what; we worship what we know. It is from the Jews that salvation comes. But the time is coming, indeed it is already here, when the true worshippers will worship the Father in spirit and truth."

John 4:21-24

Jesus wants the Samaritan woman to understand that the Jews have the right understanding of God (which is also a lesson for those who believe all religions are equal). There are many religions because throughout history people have sought the truth in different ways. But a diversity of religions does not mean or imply the equality of religions; otherwise, Jesus would not have said:

You Samaritans worship you know not what; we worship what we know. It is from the Jews that salvation comes.

John 4:22

Jesus teaches that one path is preferable to another path. We are on earth to find it.

Note again Jesus' words to the woman at the well:

"Believe me," said Jesus, "the time is coming when you will worship the Father neither on this mountain nor in Jerusalem."

John 4:21

"But the time is coming, indeed it is already here, when the true worshippers will worship the Father in spirit and truth. These are the worshippers the Father wants. God is spirit, and those who worship him must worship in spirit and truth."

John 4:23-24

That was Jesus' reply after the woman had told him:

"Our fathers worshipped on this mountain, but you Jews say that the place where God must be worshipped is in Jerusalem."

John 4:20

In a world with different holy mountains and holy places, disagreements continue to occupy the minds of many. Think of Jerusalem's Holy Sepulcher, the church built over the traditional site of Jesus' resurrection, where one Christian sect fights another – at times physical fights – over who controls what part of the Holy Sepulcher. And the world knows what a flashpoint Jerusalem is for Israelis and Muslims. In history, kings have sent armies to war over the control of holy shrines, and yet Jesus said, **"the time is coming, indeed it is already here, when the true worshippers will worship the Father in spirit and in truth."**

John 4:23

There are indeed holy mountains and shrines, but it seems that God appears less interested with a particular mountain than how He is worshipped. Worshipping in spirit and truth can be done at the North Pole or the South Pole or any point in between. Jesus' teachings are so advanced that after 2,000 years his lessons continue to challenge the world. If we understood what Jesus taught about the "true worshippers" that God seeks would Christians be fighting in Jerusalem over shrines? Or would some Israelis plan to rebuild the Temple in Jerusalem to resume sacrificial offerings? Do not mistake what I am saying: Yes, there are holy places, but Jesus taught that more important than the place of worship is the person who worships:

But the time is coming, indeed it is already here, when the true worshippers will worship the Father in spirit and in truth. These are the worshippers the Father wants.

John 4:23

Two overarching ideas are here: the first is that salvation is from the Jews and the second is that true worshippers of God worship God in spirit and truth. These two ideas are wrapped within two moral lessons for Jews and Samaritans. For Jews, the lesson was that while they looked down on Samaritans for practicing only a basic Judaism, it was the Samaritan who correctly understood the meaning of neighbor. And Jesus' lesson for the Samaritans was that salvation is also for them and it is from the Jews.

79 Man, who appointed Me a judge or arbitrator over you?
Luke 12:14 (NASB)

> Someone in the crowd said to Him, "Teacher, tell my brother to divide the *family* inheritance with me," But He said to him, "Man, who appointed Me a judge or arbitrator over you?"
> **Luke 12:13-14 (NASB)**

THIS is one of Jesus' most *astonishing* questions. Why do I say that? Remember this is the same Jesus who knew what the apostle Nathanael was doing when Nathanael was far away and out of sight. The same Jesus who knew Judas would betray him before he betrayed him. The same Jesus who brings the dead back to life.

Yet this same Jesus declines a simple request, not a request for a miracle, but only a request to intervene with wise advice to a man's brother to divide the family assets. So the Messiah who had worked miracles and came to save the entire nation of Israel would not decide a simple matter about a legacy. Why didn't he do as the man requested?

Was it because Jesus was too busy healing the sick or did Jesus think the man's request was too trifling?

I don't believe it was for those reasons. I think it was because the man's request revealed something about the man. I believe this because one notices that after Jesus asked the man, "who appointed Me a judge or arbitrator over you?" he began teaching about avarice and warned about greed: "Beware, and be on your guard against every form of greed." (Luke 12:15 NASB) He went on to warn about anxiety, that life is more than food and the body more than clothes. He talked about setting the mind toward the kingdom and the rest will come to you.

The man wanted a favorable pronouncement about his inheritance, but, instead, the man heard Jesus talk about selling possessions and giving to charity, because "not *even* when one has an abundance does his life consist of his possessions." (Luke 12:15 NASB) Jesus was less concerned with the man's inheritance on earth than the man's inheritance in heaven, which the man was in danger of losing by focusing on personal property.

> ## 80 Do you suppose I came to grant peace on earth? I tell you, no, but rather division.
> ### Luke 12:51 (NASB)

I have come to cast fire upon the earth; and how I wish it were already kindled! But I have a baptism to undergo, and how distressed I am until it is accomplished! Do you suppose I came to grant peace on earth? I tell you, no, but rather division.
Luke 12:49-51 (NASB)

Jesus' words in Matthew's version (10:34 NASB) are even harsher: "Do not think I came to bring peace on earth; I did not come to bring peace, but a sword." Jesus says he came to set a man against his father, daughter against her mother, and in-law against in-law. Jesus warns everyone where their opponents will be found, "a man's enemies will be members of his own household." (Matthew 10:36 NASB)

This, some may think, does not sound like Jesus the peacemaker, and they are troubled to hear Jesus say he wants to bring fire and a sword because those words seems to conflict with the peaceful Jesus who gave sight to the blind and forgave the repentant. And we know Jesus was not an advocate of war with Rome, so why does he say he wants to bring fire and a sword to the world?

Imagined conflicts in Jesus' teachings vanish when we remember who Jesus is and his mission. He is the Son of God and his mission is to inaugurate the Kingdom of Heaven on earth. But Satan opposes the arrival of the Kingdom of Heaven and has no intention of giving up his earthly kingdom, his kingdom of lies. No, the Enemy will have to be defeated, thus, conflict is inevitable, yet the Messiah has been given all power in Heaven and on Earth and has already overcome the world. (See Matthew 28:18 and John 16:33)

Jesus' question: "Do you suppose I came to grant peace on earth?" recognizes the reality of the conflict between truth and lies, good and evil. The conflict will end only when God's Kingdom comes in complete triumph. Jesus said he wished that the final triumph and Judgment were already happening.

> **I have come to cast fire upon the earth; and how I wish it were already kindled!**
> **Luke 12:49 (NASB)**

He has come to bring fire and the sword to the earth, but this is not to be understood as military forces. Armies are for political leaders and politicized religions, whose kingdoms are of this world.

81 Why do you not know how to interpret the present time?

Luke 12:56 RSV

You hypocrites! You know how to interpret the appearance of earth and sky; but why do you not know how to interpret the present time?

Luke 12:56 RSV

This Q tells us Jesus wants us to *observe* and to *understand*. Jewish leaders demand signs, but Jesus tells them to see signs in front of them and he wonders why they seem to grasp signs about approaching weather, but cannot see the signs of the approaching Kingdom of God.

Jewish religious leaders put Jesus to the test and want proof he is the Messiah, but it is their own understanding being tested by the presence of the Messiah as the Messiah's presence also tests the world.

82 Why can you not judge for yourselves what is right?

Luke 12:57

Why can you not judge for yourselves what is right? When you are going with your opponent to court, make an effort to reach a settlement with him while you are still on the way; otherwise he

**may drag you before the judge, and the judge hand
you over to the officer, and the officer throw you
into jail. I tell you, you will not be let out until you
have paid the last penny.**

Luke 12:57-59

Why can you not judge for yourselves what's right?

This parable is about us. We are the guilty party who is being brought
to court. What are we being charged with? Following our ancestor's
opposition to the Creator.

There may be readers who are not Christian and they may wonder
what crimes they have committed? Perhaps they think, "I generally
live honestly and, as far as I see, I am a better person than many of the
so-called Christians. So explain why I am guilty, and why, according
to your Christianity, I will be dragged to some imaginary court?"

People like to contrast themselves favorably with others – that is
human nature – and Jesus warned us against doing that. Jesus told of
a Pharisee who prayed at the Temple and thanked God he was not like
the rest of humanity, and most especially, not like the tax collector
who prayed near him. (See Luke 18:11) But after both men left the
Temple, Jesus said it was not the Pharisee, but rather the sincerely
repentant tax collector who left with his sins forgiven.

Acknowledging our selfishness and our less than honorable intentions
is difficult, but we are not really good. We know Jesus, the Son of God,
did not allow himself to be called "good." When a man said to Jesus,
"Good Teacher," Jesus replied, "Why do you call me good? No one is
good except God alone." (Luke 18:19) If the Son of God does not allow
himself to be called "good," then our own moral standing is pretty clear.

"Some may say, "I can accept I am not good; but I still ask, what am
I guilty of?"

Paul has an answer in his writings to the Romans:

There is none righteous, not even one.

Romans 3:10 (NASB)

For all have sinned and fall short of the glory of God.

Romans 3:23 (NASB)

And David answers that question in the Psalms:

Against You, You only, I have sinned
And done what is evil in your sight,
So that You are justified when you speak
And blameless when You judge

Psalm 51:4-5 (NASB)

The Lord has looked down from heaven upon the
sons of men
To see if there are any who understand,
Who seek after God.
They have all turned aside, together they have
become corrupt;
There is no one who does good, not even one.

Psalm 14:2-3 (NASB)

Proverbs also answers:

Who can say, "I have cleansed my heart, I am pure
from my sin"?

Proverbs 20:9 (NASB)

And again Paul in Romans:

What then? Are we better than they? Not at all;
for we have already charged both Jews and Greeks
are all under sin.

Romans 3:9 (NASB)

It always goes back to the beginning, back to Genesis, to Adam and Eve, to our earliest blood relations who lost friendship with God because they believed the Enemy's half-truths. Adam and Eve ignored God's warnings about the Tree of Knowledge of Good and Evil, and since that time, humans have been subject to the deceptions of the Enemy.

Christians well understand the issues of the Fall, but let us condense them for our non-Christian friends, who may know, but perhaps not grasp this part of Genesis.

Adam and Eve acted in defiance of God's order – they were persuaded by an enemy of God to disobey God, and in doing so, became part of the rebellion against God – whether passively or actively. They immediately recognized they had been lied to and as a consequence of believing that lie, they had committed an offense against God by acting against God's direct instructions.

Adam and Eve had been friends with God and they were created to live in complete harmony with His world, with mastery over themselves and the Earth; but after the rebellion, they were doomed to live in disharmony with God's world. They had committed the Original Sin.

It is noteworthy that while Judaism does not have the concept of Original Sin, rabbis do have a related concept of the *yetzer ha-ra* – an evil inclination. Both this *yetzer ha-ra* and the *yetzer ha-tov* – the good inclination – are believed by religious Jews to enter into each human after birth.

After the Fall, after their Original Sin, Adam and Eve could now suffer pain and had to struggle to gain control over themselves; they struggled with the yetzer ha-ra, the evil inclination, which had infected them and their offspring Cain and Able, and to Cain's offspring, and to you and me. This did not mean that all humans were now completely evil, but humans, after gaining knowledge of good and evil, were no longer in harmony with God or His creation. Humans still had a "good impulse" – the yetzer ha-tov, but it was weakened by the counter evil impulse.

So if some ask, "What am I guilty of before God," we Christians know the answer. If you are human, your blood condemns you because our ancestors broke with the Creator. One is free to accept this basic Truth or not. But if you do not, then I ask you – have you read today's news? Please explain today's news, if you do not think humans are morally defective. Because we see humans – whether rich or poor, healthy or sick, of this or that racial stock or ethnic group, or with an average mind or gifted intelligence – seem to be in an interminable struggle with evil. How else do you explain unceasing news about human viciousness, violence, deception, arrogance, selfishness, hate, theft and murder? What is your explanation? How do you explain all human history? And please do not suppose you have solved the mystery of evil with Marxist theories; Karl Marx not only failed to understand economics, but he failed to understand history, and not only history, but he did not comprehend the greater subject: human nature. Peoples and nations have tried Marx's ideas and variations of it, and they have not solved evil in the world, instead, they have multiplied it.

Jesus' parable of reaching a settlement before going to court presents the ominous possibility that without a settlement, Jesus said the officer can throw you into jail, and

"I tell you, you will not be let out until you have paid the very last penny." (Luke 12:59)

This has portentous implications if we understand these words to refer to judgment and the afterlife, and tells us the guilty person (us) who has not reached a settlement and made an accounting for their offences (repentance) before they are brought before the judge

(God), will go to jail and will not be released until they have paid every bit owed (just punishment for not living in harmony with God's Law). However, if hell is eternal, then paying a fine would be useless, because release is impossible. Thus, hell does not seem to be the "jail" Jesus refers to. So what could he mean that there is no release, "until you have paid the last penny"? There are Christians who take Jesus' parable to speak of an intermediate state after death, something between heaven and hell, a purgatory, a reality that is not hell, but some kind of an existence where final purification takes place before one can enter into the presence of the Holy God.

The existence of a purgatory is a grim concept rejected by many Christian churches, while it is accepted by others, who find in Luke's passage, and in related passages of the Old and New Testaments, support for their purgatorial beliefs. I do not mention this controversial subject to generate disagreement, as we have other things to think about here. But I want you to be aware that this is one of the Scriptural starting points for the viewpoint that anticipates the existence of a purgatory. It is an interesting question, but it is not, I think, on the same level of importance as what Jesus taught about how followers should live.

83 Do you suppose that, because these Galileans suffered this fate, they must have been greater sinners than anyone else in Galilee?

Luke 13:2

At that time some people came and told him about the Galileans whose blood Pilate had mixed with their sacrifices. He answered them, "Do you

**suppose that, because these Galileans suffered
this fate, they must have been greater sinners
than anyone else in Galilee? No, I tell you; but
unless you repent, you will all of you come to the
same end. Or the eighteen people who were killed
when the tower fell on them at Siloam – do you
imagine they must have been more guilty than all
the other people living in Jerusalem? No, I tell you;
but unless you repent, you will all come to an end
like theirs."**

Luke 13:1-5

In 2011, a powerful storm ripped several U.S. southern states causing
329 deaths, with 238 dead in Alabama alone. Also in 2011, an
earthquake measured as the fourth most powerful in modern history
hit Japan – the Great East Japan Earthquake – and caused over
15,000 deaths, and generated a 133 foot tsunami that swept inland
several miles and took people out to sea never to be seen again. This
earthquake was so powerful that it shifted the Earth on its axis by
an estimated 4-10 inches.

When we read about massive disasters we reflect about the victims.
Why did they meet this horrible death? Were they somehow worse in
God's eyes to suffer in an earthquake or plane crash or other terrible
fate? What would Jesus have to say about these disasters?

People in Jesus' time also wondered about disasters, and they
asked Jesus about the falling tower that killed people and of the
people in Galilee who had their blood mixed with their sacrifices by
Pilate. Jesus responded with a question: Do you think these people
were worse sinners than all the other Galileans? Or the victims in
Jerusalem were guiltier than other Jerusalemites? "No," said Jesus,
"But unless you repent, you will all come to an end like theirs." Jesus
seems to say we should not speculate about the guilt of people who
die in disasters, or wonder if they were more evil than others. Jesus'

question points to the Biblical truth that all are guilty before God. Toward the end of his mission in Israel Jesus told people what they must do to avoid dying in their sins.

> "Therefore I said to you that you will die in your sins; for unless you believe that I am *He*, you will die in your sins." (John 8:24 NASB)

84 Why should it go on taking goodness from the soil?

Luke 13:7

For the last three years I have come looking for fruit on this fig tree without finding any. Cut it down. Why should it go on taking goodness from the soil?

Luke 13:7

Another translation says, "Cut it down! Why should it be wasting the soil?" (Luke 13:7, NRSV) and another, "Why should it exhaust the soil?" (Luke 13:7, NAB) and another, "Cut it down: why should it be taking up the ground?" (Luke 13:7, NJB) *Wasting the soil, exhausting the soil, taking up ground* – translations use different phrases, but each compares humans who do not produce good works to nonproductive trees that disappoint the orchard's owner – the owner being a metaphor for God.

> **But he replied, "Leave it, sir, for this one year, while I dig around it and manure it. And if it bears fruit next season, well and good; and if not, you shall have it down."**
>
> **Luke 13:8-9**

This parable compares Jesus to a gardener asking the orchard's owner for one more year to bring the tree into fruitfulness, and if they fail to produce, he will destroy and replace them with more productive trees. The parable tells us the time to produce good works is limited and that we are currently on an extension of mercy, asked for by Jesus from his Father. Just as Noah knew time was limited before the flood, and Lot knew time was limited before Sodom's destruction, and the time was limited before Rome would destroy Jerusalem and its people – we too know the time is short.

Earth faces global destruction – the Genesis flood and destruction of Sodom and Gomorrah were regional disasters, but the Earth continued. The future global disaster will involve all life on Earth.

In this parable of the gardener, Jesus intercedes for us just as Abraham and Moses had pleaded with God to spare humans from punishment. When God planned to destroy Sodom and Gomorrah for their evil, Abraham pleaded with God not to destroy those cities if ten innocent men could be found living in them. Later in the Bible, when the Hebrews fashioned the golden bull-calf idol, God planned to destroy every Hebrew and begin a new line of Chosen people from Moses: **"Now then let Me alone, that My anger may burn against them and that I may destroy them; and I will make of you a great nation."** (Exodus 32:10 NASB) Moses pled with the God of Israel not to destroy the Israelites. The Lord heard Moses' advocacy for the people and descendents of those Hebrews live today in Israel and among the nations.

Jesus' imagery of the fruitless trees reminds us of John the Baptist's preaching:

> **The axe is already laid at the foot of the trees; therefore every tree that does not bear good fruit is cut down and thrown into the fire.**
> **Matthew 3:10 (NASB)**

We also remember the Sermon on the Mount, where the Messiah's words echo the Baptist's:

> **A good tree cannot produce bad fruit, nor can a bad tree produce good fruit. Every tree that does not bear good fruit is cut down and thrown into the fire.**
>
> **Matthew 7:18-19 (NASB)**

The judgment of God is certain, but God's judgment has been mercifully delayed. Whether that delay in judgment is only a delay or an actual acquittal is to be determined by each individual who must decide to produce good works.

> **85 Were there not ten cleansed? But the nine - where are they?**
>
> **Luke 17:17 (NASB)**

> **Then Jesus answered and said, "Were there not 10 cleansed? But the nine—where are they? Was no one found to return to give glory to God, except this foreigner?"**
>
> **Luke 17:17-18 (NASB)**

Jesus is travelling the borderlands between Galilean Jews and the Samaritans and as he reaches one village 10 lepers see him, but keep their distance, and yell out, "Jesus, Master, have mercy on us."

"Go and show yourselves to the priests," he tells them.

> Luke 17:13-14 (NASB)

They go but probably wonder why, because it was, after all, the priests who had inspected them and marked them unclean.

The Bible offers no details about their reaction to being cleansed of leprosy; I imagine they would have been ecstatic, knowing they could once again see their family and friends. The Samaritan knew what he had to do first – so he turns back and shouting praise to God, throws himself at Jesus' feet and thanks him.

The Master asks,

> **Were there not 10 cleansed? But the nine—where are they? Was no one found to return to give glory to God, except this foreigner?**
>
> **And He said to him, "Stand up and go; your faith has made you well."**
> **Luke 17:17-19 (NASB)**

Two thoughts, the first is Jesus' words that a prophet is honored, except among his family and relations and in his hometown. So we see here, nine of the 10 who had been healed were Jews, but those nine did not return and thank their fellow Jew; it was only the foreigner who thought to return and thank Jesus.

Second thought: this story shows the Jewishness of Jesus, who tells the lepers, even before their cure is manifest, to "go and show yourselves to the priests," as Jesus knew Deuteronomy instructed Jews to rely on priests to determine uncleanliness:

> **Be careful against an infection of leprosy, that you diligently observe and do according to all that the Levitical priests teach you; as I have commanded them, so you shall be careful to do.**
> **Deuteronomy 24:8 (NASB)**

Leviticus has instructions for examinations of contamination in individuals and their clothing, specifying isolation for seven days before a reexamination, and if the priest determined the individual was unclean, they were separated from community life. If the person was healed of infectious disease, as Jesus had healed these lepers, there were a number of ceremonial actions, including offerings of birds, lambs, and flour and oil, and the blood of the lamb for ceremonial guilt offerings. The priest who pronounced that the individual was clean would present them and their offerings before the Lord. Jesus knew all this when he told the 10 lepers to, **"Go and show yourselves to the priests."**

Note: Biblical leprosy was not the same disease that is today known by that name; rather, Biblical leprosy was one of a number of severe skin diseases, but that does not lessen the miracle, Luke's report, or what we can learn from it.

> **86 However, when the Son of Man comes, will he find faith on earth?**
> **Luke 18:8 (NASB)**

now, will not God bring about justice for His elect who cry to Him day and night, and will He delay long over them? I tell you that He will bring about justice for them quickly. However, when the Son of Man comes, will He find faith on earth?

Luke 18:7-8 (NASB)

God's justice is promised to those who have been denied it, to victims of violence, to those who have been repressed, tyrannized, and terrorized, to those who have been treated cruelly, ridiculed, had money and land stolen from them, their husbands, wives, and children taken away, and those who have been discriminated against without cause. All those who have suffered injustice, God hears and Jesus assures them, "I tell you that He will bring about justice for them quickly."

The second part of this question is alarming, disturbing, and unexpected for Christians.

However, when the Son of Man comes, will he find faith on earth?

How much more promising if Jesus had said something like: "When I return, *I will find* abundant faith on earth," but he did not, rather, he asked if he would find faith. His question tells us faith is difficult and it will be tested. And so, after centuries of religious debates, prophecies, prophets, evangelization, and missionary work of Christians, will the Son of Man find faith among the people or empty pews and abandoned churches? Will he find faith in the Truth or in political, philosophical, and esoteric ideologies? Will he find worship of God or of humans? While we do not know, it is our own faith we can increase and strengthen. After calming the storm, Jesus asked his men, "Where is your faith?" When he returns, will he ask us the same question?

87 Yes; have you never read, "Out of the mouth of infants and nursing babies You have prepared praise for yourself"?
Matthew 21:16 (NASB)

But when the chief priests and the scribes had seen the wonderful things that He had done, and

the children who were shouting in the temple, "Hosanna to the Son of David," they became indignant and said to Him, "Do you hear what these *children* are saying?" Jesus said to them, "Yes; have you never read, "Out of the mouths of infants and nursing babies You have prepared praise for yourself"?

Matthew 21:15-17 (NASB)

We see here parallel New Testament themes: ordinary people welcome Jesus, while the educated leaders reject him. Jesus' responds to the criticisms of the scribes and Pharisees by quoting from Psalms (See 8:2) and The Wisdom of Solomon (See 10:21). The religious leaders know the Holy texts well, but Jesus of Nazareth knows them better, but even more importantly, Jesus' understanding of Torah goes beyond knowing the words, he knows the true meaning of Torah.

88 If any one asks you, "Why are you untying it?" you shall say this, "The Lord has need of it."

Luke 19:31 RSV

Go into the village opposite, where on entering you will find a colt tied, on which no one has ever yet sat; untie it and bring it here. If anyone asks you, "Why are you untying it?" you shall say this, "The Lord has need of it."

Luke 19:30-31 RSV

Jesus had visited Jerusalem both as a boy and as an adult. He knew Jerusalem's sights and sounds, he knew of the priests, Pharisees, and he knew of the Romans, who ensured public order and respect for

Caesar. But this time his visit to Jerusalem would be much different. This time a visit from this miracle-working rabbi from Nazareth would generate shock waves through Jerusalem.

Jesus and his men had been in seclusion near the desert town of Ephraim. Their seclusion was necessary since the raising of Lazarus, the news of which alarmed the Jewish leaders: **"What are we doing? For this man is performing many signs. If we let Him *go on* like this, all men will believe in Him, and the Romans will come and take away both our place and our nation."** (John 11:47-48 NASB) Jesus' rapidly growing popularity meant the people might proclaim him King of Israel, a status that required Roman approval, and without it, proclaiming anyone to be king would mean war with Rome.

Israel's religious leaders viewed Jesus as a *religious challenge*, but if they could frame his popularity as a *political problem* they could call for Rome's intervention. So the chief priests and Pharisees convened the Sanhedrin, the court of 71 sages, at which the High Priest Caiaphas led the Sanhedrin to a decision: this teacher and miracle worker, Jesus from Galilee, was dangerous and must receive the death sentence. His popularity threatened their status, power, and position. They had been approved by Rome and they needed to ensure Jesus would be rejected by Rome. Jesus' teachings were unacceptable to the religious leaders and his interpretations of the Law always seemed to place the leadership in a negative light. While Jews respected their religious leaders, Jesus frequently seemed to criticize the leaders and the traditions that they taught.

Speculation sped through Jerusalem: Where was Jesus of Nazareth? What was this rabbi doing? Would he be in Jerusalem for Passover? Many had heard him preach in the Temple. People – always a few and usually a crowd – always surrounded him.

Jesus was the focus of a thousand conversations in Jerusalem, and I imagine one of them might have been like this.

"I heard that Jesus raised a dead man named Lazarus back to life!"

"A dead man! Is this true?"

"I heard it from my brother's friend, he was there – and he saw it with his own eyes!"

"I've heard the chief priest has ordered anyone who knows Jesus' whereabouts must inform him – so he can arrest him!"

"Arrest him? Arrest him for what? No, Jesus is a good man, they just want to talk with him."

"Remember Ozer who died last week? He owed some Pharisees a lot of money, maybe they hope Jesus can bring Ozer back to life so they can collect what he owes them."

"Don't joke about this. If his power is from God, maybe he can defeat the Romans and send them back to Rome. Maybe he is our Messiah."

"Maybe the Pharisees also think he is the Messiah, and they want to conduct an inquiry to find out – then we will all know for certain – if he is the Messiah or a false prophet."

"The young Pharisee Zivan, he is a good customer of mine, and he told me Jesus has enemies among the Pharisees because they think Jesus' attacks on traditions are outrageous. After all, Jesus is not an educated Pharisee."

"And what does Zivan think about Jesus?"

"He said – and he told me not to repeat this – but he told me he thinks Jesus is a holy man – a prophet!"

"We already know he's a prophet!"

"Yes, you are right, a prophet, certainly. But is he the Messiah?"

The raising of Lazarus was the last straw for Jewish leaders and now Jesus must be dealt with. Pharisees and Sadducees are not sure who Jesus of Nazareth is and they speculate: maybe he's a magician or maybe he has a pact with strange powers, but whoever he is, he doesn't respect us, so he must be dealt with before the people become an emotional mob and recklessly declare Jesus the King of the Jews, something the Romans would not view with calm disinterest.

Jesus left Ephraim and he was now at the Mount of Olives, a short distance outside of the huge walls surrounding Jerusalem. Before entering Jerusalem, he sends two apostles to find a colt that had never been ridden. They are to bring it back and if anyone asks why they are untying and taking it, they are to say, "The Lord has need of it." (Luke 19:31 RSV)

His arrival into Jerusalem has elements and hints of a king's royal arrival. He is escorted into the city by cheering crowds who carpet the road with their cloaks and cut palm branches and lay them in his path. Jesus goes to the Temple and acts with a king's authority, demanding those unfit to be in the Temple to leave, and uses force to ensure obedience.

Five centuries earlier, with clear prophetic sight, Zechariah saw the Messiah arrive in Jerusalem:

> **Rejoice greatly, O daughter of Zion!**
> **Shout *in triumph*, O daughter of Jerusalem!**

191

> **Behold, your king is coming to you;**
> **He is just and endowed with salvation,**
> **Humble, and mounted on a donkey,**
> **Even on a colt, the foal of a donkey.**
> **Zechariah 9:9 (NASB)**

Crowds shouted David's 118th Psalm as they walked along, and accompanied Jesus as he rode the colt:

> **Hosanna! Blessed is he who comes in the name of the Lord; Blessed *is* the coming kingdom of our father David; Hosanna in the highest!**
> **Mark 11:9-10 (NASB)**

Jesus of Nazareth saw beyond the welcoming, enthusiastic crowds that day and saw a horrifying future for Jerusalem.

> **When He approached *Jerusalem*, He saw the city and wept over it, saying, "If you had known in this day, even you, the things which make for peace! But now they have been hidden from your eyes. For days will come upon you when your enemies will throw up a barricade against you, and surround you and hem you in on every side, and they will level you to the ground and your children within you, and they will not leave in you one stone upon another, because you did not recognize the time of your visitation."**
> **Luke 19:41-44 (NASB)**

And so it was 40 years later that Roman legions surrounded and destroyed Jerusalem, its temple, and starved and killed its inhabitants. No doubt many of those who were alive when Jesus entered Jerusalem that day would have still been living, and certainly many would have remembered Jesus' words.

89 The Teacher says, "Where is the room in which I am to eat the Passover with my disciples?"

Luke 22:11

Then came the day of the Unleavened Bread, on which the Passover lambs had to be slaughtered, and Jesus sent off Peter and John, saying, "Go and prepare the Passover supper for us." "Where would you like us to make the preparations?" they asked. He replied, "As soon as you set foot in the city a man will meet you carrying a jar of water. Follow him into the house that he enters and give this message to the householder: 'The Teacher says, "Where is the room in which I am to eat the Passover with my disciples?"' He will show you a large room upstairs all set out: make the preparations there." They went out and found everything as he had said. So they prepared for Passover.

Luke 22:7-13

Natural explanations cannot explain Jesus knowing how Peter and John would find a room for Passover. One can speculate, "Perhaps Jesus knew the man with the jar of water, and had previously arranged for him to meet Peter and John."

Maybe, but if that were true, why did Jesus appear unconcerned about *where* in the city Peter and John needed to go to meet the man with a jar, thus leaving their meeting to chance? In fact, Jesus told Peter and John they would meet the man carrying a jar of water, "as soon as you set foot in the city," as if there was no possibility Peter and John would not meet him.

This is another case where Jesus shows perception beyond ordinary humans. We earlier read where Jesus foretold the destruction of Jerusalem and accurately described Roman tactics that they would use 40 years in the future. If he could see that far into the future, it is reasonable that he had the ability to see the near future, and see how the two disciples would find a room for Passover.

Others might read Luke's passage and say, "Maybe Jesus had psychic powers." Many people have a sixth sense and who hasn't had the odd experience of sensing someone was about to call just before they did, or the experience of thinking of someone just before they turn a corner and bump into them. These are common experiences.

But Jesus' power was more significant than psychic talent and we see it at other times. Remember Jesus telling Peter: "Truly, I tell you: before the cock crows you will disown me three times." (Matthew 26:34)

We experience daily events in order, in a sequence, a logical progression. We remember events that have occurred and describe them as having happened in the past and although we can imagine the future it is vague and uncertain.

When the Messiah speaks of the future, it is beyond psychic talent. I believe it is because *he is the Messiah*. Our experiences are limited by time, but God is unlimited and since Jesus is one with the Father, he would also in some way be unlimited by time. As he said in John:

> **"Your father Abraham rejoiced to see My day; and he *saw it* and was glad." So the Jews said to Him, "You are not yet fifty years old, and have You seen Abraham? Jesus said to them, "Truly, truly, I say to you, before Abraham was born, I am."**
>
> **John 8:56-58 (NASB)**

Even the simple matter of finding a room to celebrate Passover reveals the divinity of the Messiah.

90 For who is greater – the one who sits at table or the servant who waits on him?
Luke 22:27

> **For who is greater – the one who sits at table or the servant who waits on him? Surely the one who sits at table. Yet I am among you like a servant.**
>
> **Luke 22:27**

Jesus' words – *I am among you like a servant* – do not seem to make sense. Why would the Son of God, the King of Israel act like a servant? He said this to his disciples who had been arguing about who was the greatest. The Master said to the disciples:

> **Among the Gentiles, kings lord it over their subjects; and those in authority are given the title Benefactor. Not so with you: on the contrary, the greatest among you must bear himself like the youngest, the one who rules like the one who serves.**
>
> **Luke 22.25-26**

What Jesus said makes no sense in the context of our everyday experience, but he wants to prepare the minds of his followers for the Kingdom of God, where there is justice, goodwill, and service to others.

You might view Luke's story to be about a humble servant, and it is; but at the same time it points to something unexpected. Reread

Jesus' question, **"For who is greater – the one who sits at table or the servant who waits on him? Surely the one who sits at table. Yet I am among you like a servant."**

This question reveals one of Jesus' great themes – what we can think of as the *Universal Reversal* – and Jesus taught about a *Universal Reversal* again and again using different images.

We often see the obsequious, groveling employees advance faster in their careers than those who simply work hard without being fawning toward superiors. This is less true in small family businesses where it is clear who does the work, but in large organizations and companies, we frequently see the world Jesus spoke about. **"for the sons of this age are more shrewd in relation to their own kind than the sons of light."**

Luke 16:8 (NASB)

The Kingdom of Heaven will mean a *Universal Reversal* where divine judgment reverses all injustice, inequity, and hypocrisy. Many who are now first will be last, and many who are now last will be first, Jesus said. In the Kingdom of Heaven, the hungry will be satisfied, while those who are now filled will go hungry. He said those who weep now will laugh, but those who laugh now will weep. Jesus said the humble will be exalted and the exalted will be humbled (See Luke 6:21-25 and Luke 18:14). The Universal Reversal and the Kingdom of Heaven will bring unsurpassed happiness. Blessed are those who hunger and thirst to see right prevail, they shall be satisfied, the Messiah said.

> **Now God has his dwelling with mankind! He will dwell among them and they shall be his people, and God himself will be with them.**
> **Revelation 21:3**

A new Jerusalem and a new Earth.

91 Do you understand what I have done for you?

John 13:12

After washing their feet he put on his garment and sat down again. "Do you understand what I have done for you?" he asked. "You call me Teacher and Lord, and rightly so, for that is what I am. Then if I, your Lord and Teacher, have washed your feet, you also ought to wash one another's feet. I have set you an example: you are to do as I have done for you. In very truth I tell you, a servant is not greater than his master, nor a messenger than the one who sent him. If you know this, happy are you if you act upon it.

John 13:12-17

At the Passover celebration, Jesus put on servant's clothing and washed and dried the disciples' feet with a towel, as though he were their servant. Peter objected – but Jesus told him that while Peter couldn't understand at that moment, he would one day.

The Messiah-King was rejected by the world, because our world rejects a king who does not use his power for self-aggrandizement. We expect kings and queens to be dignified and imposing, and perhaps even vain and arrogant. The King of England does not serve his servants.

Jesus was not the king the world expected.

Judas would have seen Jesus wash the disciple's feet and his own. What did Judas do after he saw the foot washing? He left them to betray them. Was seeing Jesus do servant's work what convinced Judas that the man from Nazareth was not the Messiah? Was Judas disappointed for Jesus – or for himself? Had Judas dreamt of being second-in-command to the Messiah? Had Judas hoped for political connections if Jesus were the King of Israel? Did Judas want a Jewish king who would grant favors, distribute money and lead armies? Perhaps Judas saw Jesus would not be a powerful king with servants, as Jesus himself acted like a servant. Did this disappoint Judas? Did the betrayer feel betrayed?

Judas may have forgotten what the Master had taught, **"Whoever exalts himself shall be humbled; and whoever humbles himself shall be exalted"?**

Matthew 23:12 (NASB)

> **92 When I sent you out barefoot without purse or pack, were you ever short of anything?**
>
> **Luke 22:35**

He said to them, "When I sent you out barefoot without purse or pack, were you ever short of anything?" "No," they answered. "It is different now," he said; "whoever has a purse had better take it with him, and his pack too; and if he has no sword, let him sell his cloak to buy one."

Luke 22:35-36

Do you remember when you were one-year old? Or three? Or four years old? Most of us forget our early years as we undergo what psychologists call infantile amnesia. But whether we remember them or not, we know our parents cared for us and helped us to grow and mature. Our parents and others met our needs for food, shelter, and family.

As we became older, our parents helped us transition to a more self-sufficient life, where we needed to think more maturely, more independently, and provide for ourselves. We learned to make decisions that were framed by the moral teachings they taught by word and example. We became adults.

This is something like what Jesus is saying here to his men: when you were children under my care, you lacked nothing, now it is different; because those parts of your lessons are ending, and you must now become adults spiritually and learn more difficult lessons.

In all of my Old and New Testaments studies, I never read of a prophet, a holy man, or Jesus of Nazareth say we should not use reason. Jesus expects us to use the common sense God gave us and develop our powers of reason to the highest level we can. The combination of experience, reason, and common sense is called wisdom. The Messiah wants us to be wise. Remember what he told his disciples: "I send you out as sheep in the midst of wolves; so be shrewd as serpents and innocent as doves."

Matthew 10:16 (NASB)

I believe Jesus of Nazareth is saying to followers: Think, prepare, make plans and pursue them with common sense and wisdom. Pray for my guidance, for the Holy Spirit, and you will receive them. Prepare yourself spiritually as well as with the necessary material assets. **"It is different now," he said; "whoever has a purse had better take it with him, and his pack too; and if he has no sword, let him sell his cloak to buy one."**

93 Jesus answered, "Do you now believe?"
John 16:31

I did not tell you this at first, because then I was with you; but now I am going away to him who sent me. None of you asks me, "Where are you going?"
John 16:4-5

Jesus knew that they were wanting to question him, and said, "Are you discussing that saying of mine: 'A little while, and you will not see me, and again a little while, and you will see me'"?
John 16:19

Jesus answered, "Do you now believe?"
John 16:31

The Messiah's teachings and popularity vex Israel's religious leaders, and with Passover, Jesus' enemies agree he must be dealt with in a definitive manner. Religious leaders order anyone aware of Jesus' whereabouts to tell them, so he can be arrested. The religious leaders are now ready to take any action – bribing informers, arresting Jesus at night, conducting a night tribunal – to ensure an end to his teachings. And religious leaders also know Jesus brought Lazarus back to life, so they also plan to murder Lazarus to erase the living proof of that miracle. The leaders want Jesus brought to a permanent stop.

Then the chief priests and the elders of the people were gathered together in the court of the high

priest, named Caiaphas, and they plotted together
to seize Jesus by stealth and kill Him.
Matthew 26:3-4 (NASB)

The leaders cannot accept that a working-class, miracle-worker from Nazareth is the Messiah. Jesus is not one of the elites. Jesus does not praise the religious elites. Jesus does not seek approval of the elites. Instead, he criticizes them, calls them hypocrites, and says they are destined for Hell, while telling them that many tax-collectors, prostitutes, and sinners have repented, believed the Good News, and are Heaven-bound.

Dark events are closing in and the trap is set. Now it is Passover and Jesus meets with his disciples for the Passover meal, knowing it is his last meal with his circle of friends. John's Gospel presents a triad of questions Jesus asks at Passover:

None of you asks me, "Where are you going?"
John 16:5

Are you discussing that saying of mine: "A little
while, and you will not see me, and again a little
while, and you will see me"?
John 16:19

Jesus answered, "Do you now believe?"
John 16:31

Jesus introduces his first question by saying he is **"going away to him who sent me," (John 16:5)** adding, **"I came from the Father and have come into the world; and now I am leaving the world again and going to the Father."**
John 16:28

The disciples are happy with Jesus' clarification: **"Now you are speaking plainly and not in figures of speech!"**
John 16:29

But only a bit earlier, when Jesus posed a second question, his disciples wondered at its meaning, **"A little while, and you will not see me, and again a little while, and you will see me."** Jesus tells them their sadness will be brief because he will see them again, **"and then you will be joyful, and no one shall rob you of your joy."**

John 16:22

After Judas leaves the Last Supper, Jesus says something astonishing:

> **You are my friends, if you do what I command you. No longer do I call you servants, for a servant does not know what his master is about. I have called you friends, because I have disclosed to you everything that I have heard from my Father.**
> **John 15:14-15**

The Messiah calls followers his *friends*. It seems illogical that the Messiah wants us as friends, we who are just short-lived creatures living on a tiny bit of God's Universe with our limited minds.

Can you imagine a politician wanting to be your friend? Perhaps, but you would wonder what they wanted from you. Or can you imagine a Hollywood celebrity wanting to be your friend; again, you might be pleased but also suspicious.

To my thinking, the Son of God offering friendship with his followers far exceeds all such unlikely possibilities.

Why would God want our friendship? He wants our friendship because He wants His creation to share His existence and love. This seems far-fetched, but it is true. This is a friendship worth developing and our present and future happiness depends upon it. Even the best of human friendships may disappoint or simply fade away overtime, but friendship with the Son of God is an eternal and true friendship.

You are my friends, if you do what I command you.
John 15:14

In offering his followers the status of "friend," he offers a status previously bestowed on Abraham himself:

But you, Israel, My servant, Jacob whom I have chosen, Descendant of Abraham My friend.
Isaiah 41:8 (NASB)

The eleven remaining disciples at last seem to grasp that Jesus of Nazareth is from God and Jesus asks them:

Do you now believe?
John 16:31

We read of some who live solitary lives in monasteries and we may think, "How odd!" Perhaps we think their lives away from society are difficult. But, maybe for them, they are spending all of their time with their best friend. Perhaps they know that the friendship between God and us, which was broken in the Garden of Eden, is now real again.

94 Will you lay down your life for Me?
John 13:38 (NASB)

Peter said to Him, "Lord, why can I not follow You right now? I will lay down my life for you." Jesus answered, "Will you lay down your life for Me?

Truly, truly, I say to you, a rooster will not crow until you deny Me three times."
John 13:37-38 (NASB)

Appointed by Jesus as first among the disciples, Peter pledges he will die for Jesus, but the Messiah asks how sure Peter is about his pledge, "Will you lay down your life for Me? Truly, truly, I say to you, a rooster will not crow until you deny Me three times." (NASB 13:38)

Like many other individuals in the Bible, Jesus will face his destiny without help from man or woman. He will be alone. Abraham's covenant with God was enacted alone. Moses went to the mountaintop to receive the commandments alone. Jacob wrestled with the angel alone. David faced Goliath alone. John the Baptist was beheaded alone. Jesus stood trial alone. At the most lonely, abandoned, and critical moments, the Bible's heroes and Holy Ones frequently have none to accompany them but God and His angels.

Are some Christians alone and outnumbered in the world today? Yes they are in some places, but even in those cases they are not abandoned, as the Holy Spirit guides the Christian community and God's angels accompany and protect His own.

Peter's human allegiance to the Messiah stalled, but the Messiah's help to his followers does not.

95 Asleep, Simon? Could you not stay awake for one hour?

Mark 14:37

He came back and found them asleep; and he said to Peter, "Asleep, Simon? Could you not stay awake for one hour? Stay awake, all of you; and pray that you may be spared the test. The spirit is willing, but the flesh is weak." Once more he went away and prayed. On his return he found them asleep again, for their eyes were heavy; and they did not know how to answer him.

He came a third time and said to them, "Still asleep? Still resting? Enough! The hour has come. The Son of Man is betrayed into the hands of sinners. Up, let us go! The traitor is upon us."

Mark 14:37-42

As Jesus' arrest and torture and death close in, Mark's Gospel describes Jesus' agony:

"My soul is deeply grieved to the point of death; remain here and keep watch."

Mark 14:34 (NASB)

In his distress he asks his friends to help him petition God, but they are exhausted. There was an earlier event that mirrors this one. Remember? While in this instance Jesus asks his men to stay awake, in the earlier event, the disciples wanted Jesus to wake from sleep. Remember on the Sea of Galilee when his men were sinking in the storm? Jesus woke from sleep to save them, but now as the storm gathers around Jesus, his men continue sleeping.

Another mirror image, Jesus of Nazareth began his mission alone and praying in the wilderness, where the enemy tried to divert him from his destiny. Now Jesus ends his mission alone and praying, as the enemy inspires evil men to end his life. Jesus both begins and ends his mission in prayer, with evil always opposing him.

96 Whom do you seek?
John 18:4 (NASB)

So Jesus, knowing all the things that were coming upon Him, went forth and said to them, "Whom do you seek?"

John 18:4 (NASB)

Therefore He again asked them, "Whom do you seek?" And they said, "Jesus the Nazarene."

John 18:7 (NASB)

Jesus' question is not only for the soldiers, but it is an enduring question for the world.

Jesus' question, "Whom do you seek?" is imprinted throughout the New Testament.

"Who is it?" the Magi were looking for in Bethlehem? "Who is it?" Herod wanted to kill by ordering the death of every infant in Bethlehem? "Who is it?" that Simon, the Temple holy man, wanted to hold when he saw Mary and Joseph with their infant? "Who is it?" The Baptist was preparing the way for? "Who is it" who stood before High Priest Caiaphas?

Who is it the world is looking for now? A politician? A scientist? A philosopher? A world leader?

97 Have you come out with swords and clubs to arrest Me as *you would* against a robber?
Matthew 26:55 (NASB)

At that time Jesus said to the crowds, "Have you come out with swords and clubs to arrest Me as *you would* against a robber? Every day I used to sit in the temple teaching and you did not seize me."
Matthew 26:55 (NASB)

Evil favors darkness – Jesus is arrested at night as though he were a criminal, while he had taught in daylight in the temple day after day, but his enemies come at night.

"For everyone who does evil hates the Light, and does not come to the Light for fear that his deeds will be exposed."
John 3:20 (NASB)

98 Do you suppose that I cannot appeal for help to my Father, and at once be sent more than twelve legions of angels?
Matthew 26:53

Do you suppose that I cannot appeal for help to my Father, and at once be sent more than twelve legions

of angels? But how then would the scriptures be fulfilled, which say that this must happen?
Matthew 26:53-54

If Heaven's legions are the same size as Rome's legions, 12 legions would be 62,880 angels, and Jesus said if he asked for help his Father would have sent that many angels and more. At the last supper just hours earlier, Jesus declared the world's ruler was powerless over him, **"the prince of the world approaches. He has no rights over me."** (John 14:30) Even though the world has no power over the Messiah, he still suffered according to God's will. The three questions Jesus asked at this pivotal moment share the same meaning: Jesus will follow the will of the Father.

But how then would the scriptures be fulfilled, which say that this must happen?
Matthew 26:54 (see following, John 12:27-28)

Now my soul is in turmoil, and what am I to say? "Father, save me from this hour"? No, it was for this that I came to this hour. Father, glorify your name.
John 12:27-28

So Jesus said to Peter, "Put the sword into the sheath; the cup which the Father has given Me, shall I not drink it?"
John 18:11 (NASB)

99 How then will the Scriptures be fulfilled, *which say* that it must happen this way?

Matthew 26:54 (NASB)

Or do you think that I cannot appeal to My Father, and He will at once put at My disposal more than twelve legions of angels? How then will the Scriptures be fulfilled, *which say* that it must happen this way?

Matthew 26:53-54 (NASB)

The Son of God is treated like an outlaw. Jesus knew what was ahead of him in the next few hours: people he had healed would desert him, religious experts would reject him, closest friends would leave him, and the Roman governor would approve his death by crucifixion. He would be tortured and put to death using a type of execution so humiliating that Rome had banned it for any Roman citizen.

One of Jesus' inner-circle was a traitor – his name is a synonymous with deceit and betrayal – after dark he led a detachment of soldiers and temple police to Jesus and his disciples. Jesus said to the arresting party, "But this is your hour – when darkness reigns." (Luke 22:53)

About thirty years earlier Jesus' father, Joseph, was warned in a dream to take his small family to Egypt because King Herod wanted to kill the newly born king of Israel. King Herod was now long dead, but his vicious goal was within reach: to kill the *real* King of the Jews. The Sanhedrin would condemn Jesus to death, and some of its senior members probably remembered that 30 years earlier Magi from the East came to Bethlehem, Israel in search of a baby boy. Some of the older Sanhedrin members probably remembered that when the Magi did not tell Herod where they had found the infant, an enraged Herod ordered every baby boy in Bethlehem two-years of age or younger put to death.

Did any member of the Sanhedrin wonder if Jesus could be the child Herod sought to kill? If so, they probably thought, "No, this is Jesus of Nazareth – not Jesus of Bethlehem!" Perhaps thinking any baby boy born in Bethlehem 30 years ago would not have survived King Herod's order. But Jesus did survive.

Herod wanted to kill the king of the Jews and Herod's evil spirit lived on in others, even though the Sanhedrin was unaware they were being inspired by it. Evil pursues it goals though various men at various times down through history. Evil has victories, but each victory ultimately turns into defeat. Each defeat of Christ's followers is temporary and turns to victory for the followers of the Messiah.

On the night of his arrest, the Messiah warned his men that it was not time for the sword, and as he was being taken away as prisoner, Jesus asked:

> **Or do you think that I cannot appeal to My Father, and He will at once put at My disposal more than twelve legions of angels? How then will the Scriptures be fulfilled, *which say* that it must happen this way?**

All his men ran away while Peter followed Jesus at a distance (See Luke 22:54). Jesus would face the full force of his destiny without a friend.

Some may believe that the anguish of Jesus of Nazareth is an event of such cosmic significance, that it can have no direct relevance for them. I agree that the Messiah's suffering is of cosmic importance, but I disagree it has no direct relevance for followers.

Everyone knows injustice, suffering, and death are woven into our existence and are unavoidable. For followers of the Messiah, there will come a time when they will be alone. A time when their friends will desert them, or simply be too far away or unable to help. A time when illness will be beyond the skills of doctors, or when corrupt and powerful forces overwhelm them. There will come a time when they will be abandoned and alone, but not completely alone.

Men abandoned the Messiah, but the Messiah will not abandon his followers.

> **100 This is the cup the Father has given me; shall I not drink it?**
>
> **John 18:11**

Matthew, Mark, Luke and John all report the night of Jesus' arrest and describes what was witnessed by the Gospel author or told to him.

In Matthew, Jesus says to the disciples,

> **"Are you still sleeping and resting? Behold, the hour is at hand and the Son of Man is being betrayed into the hands of sinners."**
> **Matthew 26:45 (NASB)**

Luke writes, **"While He was still speaking, behold, a crowd *came*, and the one called Judas, one of the twelve, was preceding them; and he approached Jesus to kiss him. But Jesus said to him, "Judas, are you betraying the Son of Man with a kiss?"**
> **Luke 22:47-48 (NASB)**

> **When those who were around Him saw what was going to happen, they said, "Lord, shall we strike with the sword?" And one of them struck the slave of the high priest and cut off his right ear. But Jesus answered and said, "Stop! No more of this!" And He touched his ear and healed him.**
> **Luke 22:49-51 (NASB)**

Mark writes, **One of the bystanders drew his sword, and struck the high priest's servant, cutting off his ear. Then Jesus spoke: "Do you take me for a robber, that you have come out with swords and cudgels to arrest me? Day after day I have been among you teaching in the temple, and you did not lay hands on me. But let the scriptures be fulfilled." Then the disciples all deserted him and ran away.**

Among those who had followed Jesus was a young man with nothing on but a linen cloth. They tried to seize him; but he slipped out of the linen cloth and ran away naked.

Mark 14:47-52

John's account makes us feel like we are witnessing the arrest; even giving us the name of the high priest's servant, and only in John's Gospel does Jesus ask the soldiers and temple police a question.

After this prayer, Jesus went out with his disciples across the Kedron ravine. There was a garden there, and he and his disciples went into it. The place was known to Judas, his betrayer, because Jesus had often met there with his disciples. So Judas made his way there with a detachment of soldiers, and with temple police provided by the chief priests and the Pharisees; they were equipped with lanterns, torches, and weapons. Jesus, knowing everything that was to happen to him, stepped forward and asked them, "Who is it you want?" "Jesus of Nazareth," they answered. Jesus said, "I am he." And Judas the traitor was standing there with them. When Jesus said, "I

am he," they drew back and fell to the ground. Again he asked, "Who is it you want?" "Jesus of Nazareth," they repeated. "I have told you that I am he," Jesus answered. "If I am the man you want, let these others go." (This was to make good his words, "I have not lost one of those you gave me.") Thereupon Simon Peter drew the sword he was wearing and struck at the high priest's servant, cutting off his right ear. The servant's name was Malchus. Jesus said to Peter, "Put away your sword. This is the cup the Father has given me; shall I not drink it?"

The troops with their commander, and the Jewish police, now arrested Jesus and secured him.

John 18:1-12

Matthew, Luke, and John all record Jesus repudiating the use of force to defend him against arrest, **"Put your sword back into its place; for all those who take up the sword shall perish by the sword."** (Matthew 26:52 NASB) But didn't Jesus use force to eject the moneychangers and sellers of sacrificial animals from the Temple? Yes, he did, yet now, as Jesus is arrested, he stops Peter from defending him with force. Jesus accepts the destiny prophesized by the High Priest Caiaphas, who had spoken an unintended prophecy about Jesus to the council of priests and Pharisees:

But one of them, Caiaphas, who was high priest that year, said to them, "You know nothing at all, nor do you take into account that it is expedient for you that one man die for people, and that the whole nation not perish."

John 11:49-50 (NASB)

101 Why are you questioning me? Question those who heard me, they know what I said.

John 18:21

The high priest questioned Jesus about his disciples and about his teaching. Jesus replied, "I have spoken openly for all the world to hear; I have always taught in the synagogues or in the temple, where all Jews congregate; I have said nothing in secret. Why are you questioning me? Question those who heard me, they know what I said.

John 18:19-21

Jesus replied, "If I was wrong to speak what I did, produce evidence to prove it; if I was right, why strike me?

John 18:23

A night meeting of priests and elders is called to investigate this unusual teacher – Jesus of Nazareth. They face the worrying and urgent issue that Jesus' popularity is increasing and now they have learned the reports that Jesus has brought a man back from the dead, and this controversial man now stands before the council. The high priest inquires about his teachings and his disciples and Jesus replies he has taught in public places where many Jews gather.

I have said nothing in secret. Why are you questioning me? Question those who heard me; they know what I said.

John 18:20-21

A temple policeman is standing by and strikes Jesus, saying, **"Is that the way to answer the high priest?"** (John 18:22) Jesus replied:

If I was wrong to speak what I did, produce evidence to prove it; if I was right, why strike me?
John 18:23

It is a grievous injustice for an innocent person to be found guilty, but this trial is more terrible because not only is the innocent man found guilty, but a murderer, Barabbas, will be freed in his place. The guilty will be set free and the innocent condemned.

> How long will you judge unjustly
> And show partiality to the wicked?
> **Psalm 82:2 (NASB)**

Religious experts put God's son on trial. Our world put the witness to the Truth on trial and condemned him. Is there a greater error? Could there be a greater wrong than condemning truth? Some might think that the people at that time certainly thought that they could trust the judgment of their respected leaders. Their trust was misplaced. The Messiah went unrecognized by the experts – the same experts the people thought would tell them if the Messiah had come, especially if the Messiah was standing in front of them.

There is an eerie correspondence between Jesus and Barabbas: Jesus of Nazareth and Barabbas *had the same first name* – which is *Yehoshua* in Hebrew and *Jesus* in English.

When the people assembled Pilate said to them, "Which would you like me to release to you – Jesus Barabbas, or Jesus called Messiah?"
Matthew 27:17

And this is even more eerie: Barabbas means "son of the father." (In three different Bible translations Barabbas is identified as Jesus

Barabbas.) So, when Pilate asked whom he should release, Pilate was asking the people to choose between Jesus and Jesus. That is, between Jesus of Nazareth (the Son of God the Father) and Jesus Barabbas (son of the father). In that cosmic moment, they chose between the criminal son of an earthly father, and the innocent Son of the Heavenly Father. Between light and darkness, Holy and unholy, truth and lies, the Prince of Peace and a criminal. The people chose the criminal and as some people still do – whenever they choose lies over truth.

> **But because I speak the truth, you do not believe Me.**
> **John 8:45 (NASB)**

What did Jesus of Nazareth say to those who had pardoned a criminal and then crucified him?

> **Father, forgive them; for they do not know what they are doing.**
> **Luke 23:34 (NASB)**

102 Is that your own question, or have others suggested it to you?
John 18:34

Pilate then went back into his headquarters and summoned Jesus.

"So you are the king of the Jews?" he said.

Jesus replied, "Is that your own question, or have others suggested it to you?"

"Am I a Jew?" said Pilate. "Your own nation and their chief priests have brought you before me. What have you done?"

Jesus replied, "My kingdom does not belong to this world. If it did, my followers would be fighting to save me from the clutches of the Jews. My kingdom belongs elsewhere."

"You are a king, then?" said Pilate.

Jesus answered, "King is your word. My task is to bear witness to the truth. For this I was born; for this I came into the world, and all who are not deaf to truth listen to my voice."

Pilate said, "What is truth?"

John 18:33-38

This is the supreme and final question: What is truth? That is the question every belief system, ideology, and philosophy wants to answer. Atheists deny transcendent truth exists, but to know the ultimate truth is why we are here.

When Governor Pilate asked, "What is truth?" he was aware of Athens' great philosophers and Rome's highly regarded priests, and he probably viewed the Jews as second-rate to Rome and Athens in understanding philosophy and religion. Thus when he asked, "What is truth?" Pilate was likely challenging Jesus to see if he knew Greek philosophy, or to see if he could answer about the gods, the way Roman priests might have answered. But Jesus remained silent before the Roman.

Pilate wants facts from the prisoner: "Your own nation and your chief priests have brought you before me. What have you done?"

John 18:35

Jesus: **"My kingdom does not belong to this world."**
                                              John 18:36

A little later, after Jesus is flogged and soldiers put a crown of thorns on his head, Pilate asks: **"Where have you come from?**
                                              John 19:9

Jesus is silent.

Pilate loses patience:

"Do you refuse to speak to me?" said Pilate. "Surely you know that I have authority to release you, and authority to crucify you?"
                                              John 19:10

Jesus finally speaks, but only to correct Pilate's viewpoint:

"You would have no authority at all over me", Jesus replied, "if it had not been granted you from above; and therefore the deeper guilt lies with the one who handed me over to you."
                                              John 19:11

Jesus' answer forms the worldview of Christians and many Jews: God's power is total and His will is perfectly triumphant. Even when God's enemies successfully hinder the Will of God, their obstruction is only temporary; God's victory is assured.

What did Pilate think when Jesus said to him, **"You would have no authority at all over me, if it had not been granted you from above"**?

What does this peculiar Jew mean? I am governor because of my service and my friends in Rome. What do the gods care about me? What do they have to do with my success? I am succeeding in life because of my hard work and my influential friends. Thus Pontius Pilate was likely to have thought – as do many successful people today.

It was morning when Pilate heard the accusations against Jesus and he was unhappy to be put in the middle of a dispute concerning a religion to which he did not belong, and among a people he did not like. But entangled he was, because religious leaders wanted an end to the Jesus phenomenon; they wanted an end to Jesus' teachings, to Jesus' miracles, and to growing talk Jesus is the Messiah.

Jesus' teachings taught the true meaning of the Prophets and the Law, but the Jewish leaders disputed Jesus' teachings, seeing them as against the Law and tradition. In order to use the death penalty against Jesus of Nazareth, Rome had to be called into the dispute. Political tensions pushed in on Pilate. The governor had to decide if the Galilean was a threat to Rome or only to Israel's leaders? Was Jesus a danger or harmless? To decide, Pilate relied on his experience in Israel and the testimony he heard regarding Jesus. But all who testified, testified against Jesus and wanted one thing: Roman approval for a crucifixion.

Jesus was friendless. Pilate had seen other such abandoned prisoners, but they had usually been criminals. Pilate had himself felt the heat of Jewish hatred because he had harshly treated them, but he was perplexed to see the intensity of the hatred toward Jesus. It was strange and unworldly. It seemed to come from some other power.

Two things disturb Pilate – his wife's dream and the gods. As Pilate sat on the judgment seat, his wife sent him a message: **"Have nothing to do with that righteous Man; for last night I suffered greatly in a dream because of Him." (Matthew 27:19 NASB)**

Pilate's second concern was the chance Jesus was actually related to the gods. Pilate knew Caesars claimed to be gods, was it possible this Jew was also related to the divine? Pilate had witnessed odd customs and strange peoples, but none as mysterious as this man. What if Jesus really *was* related to the gods? If he were, Pilate knew the gods would avenge any action taken against him.

As he stood before Pilate, Jesus knew Pilate's brutal reputation. Once, while Jesus taught, he received a report Pilate had mixed Galilean blood with their sacrifices (See Luke 13:1).

Pilate came to a decision: Jesus of Nazareth was not a threat to Rome. He may have offended Jewish priests in some dubious dispute over doctrine, but Jesus had no army and no powerful friends, and therefore Jesus was insignificant to Rome. Jesus had told Pilate that, "His kingdom is not of this world," well good, Pilate probably thought, because Rome's Empire is of this world, and so long as Jesus does not interfere with Rome, he can teach and perform an occasional miracle, because this Roman governor does not care. Rome is the world's greatest power and is unconcerned with esoteric religious disputes, especially those involving a minor religion in a corner of Rome's vast Empire. Whatever doubts Pilate may have had, Pilate knew this: muscular German tribes on the Empire's borders were a threat, uncivilized Celtic tribes were a threat, mass movements of barbarian tribes were a threat – but a wandering rabbi with no soldiers or even a friend… no, Pilate thought, this man is not a threat to Rome.

Pilate now summoned the chief priests, councillors, and people, and said to them, "You brought this man before me on a charge of subversion. But, as you see, I have myself examined him in your presence and found nothing in him to support your charges. No more did Herod, for he referred him back to us. Clearly he has done nothing to deserve

death. I therefore propose to flog him and let him go." But there was a general outcry. "Away with him! Set Barabbas free! (Now Barabbas had been put in prison for his part in a rising in the city and for murder.) Pilate addressed them again, in his desire to release Jesus, but they shouted back, "Crucify him, crucify him!" For the third time he spoke to them: "Why? What wrong has he done? I have not found him guilty of any capital offense. I will therefore flog him and let him go." But they persisted with their demand, shouting that Jesus should be crucified. Their shouts prevailed, and Pilate decided that they should have their way. He released the man they asked for, the man who had been put in prison for insurrection and murder, and gave Jesus over to their will.

Luke 23:13-25

Chief Priests and Pharisees said their Law and traditions were the truth.

Romans said their law and their Empire's world power were political truth.

But when Pilate asked, "What is truth?" Jesus did not answer, although only hours earlier Jesus had answered that question at the Last Supper.

"I am the way, and the truth, and the life; no one comes to the Father but through me."

John 14:6 (NASB)

What did Pontius Pilate remember about Jesus' trial after returning to Rome? Did he remember the shouting or the silence – the shouting of the mob or the silence of Jesus?

Christians know Jesus has answered the eternal question, "What is truth?" because they accept the Bible as true, while the skeptics dismiss it as fiction. Some of these skeptics even think Pontius Pilate is fiction.

There is a beautiful museum near Hebrew University in Jerusalem containing an impressive archaeological collection, including the Dead Sea Scrolls and the world's oldest biblical manuscripts. I have been there. This museum's fine exhibits are organized in chronological order, and as I walked through the museum's section with artifacts from the period when Jesus was alive, I saw something I didn't know existed: it was a large white limestone stone which sat on the floor in an upright position. The stone was about three feet tall and two feet wide and words are carved on it in Latin. Although the words are partially destroyed, archeologists have deciphered the remaining Latin and agree it translates into English in this way:

> To the Divine Augustus this Tiberieum
> Pontius Pilate
> Prefect of Judea
> Has dedicated this …

Some skeptics won't change their minds even if the proof is carved in stone.

> **103 For if these things are done when the wood is green, what will happen when it is dry?**
>
> **Luke 23:31**

222

**Great numbers of people followed, among them
many women who mourned and lamented over
him. Jesus turned to them and said, "Daughters of
Jerusalem, do not weep for me; weep for yourselves
and your children. For the days are surely coming
when people will say, "Happy are the barren, the
wombs that never bore a child, the breasts that
never fed one." Then they will begin to say to the
mountains, "Fall on us," and to the hills, "Cover
us." For if these things are done when the wood is
green, what will happen when it is dry?**

Luke 23:27-31

Flogging was so bloody and gruesome that some men died from
the pain it inflicted. After being flogged, Jesus would have been
weak from blood loss. He stumbled as he carried the wooden cross
and Simon from Cyrene was pulled from the crowds to carry it and
walk behind the King as the condemned man from Nazareth went
to his execution. Jesus' certainly now looked nothing like what Jews
thought their Messiah should look like, but even in his tortured state,
he continued to teach the people, **"do not weep for me; weep for
yourselves and your children. For the days are surely coming
when people will say, 'Happy are the barren, the wombs that
never bore a child, the breasts that never fed one.'"**

Some of those who heard him probably understood Jesus was
fortifying his prediction of Jerusalem's future, because, just days
earlier, when he entered Jerusalem to a warm welcome, he said:

**If you had known in this day, even you, the things
which make for peace! But now they have been
hidden from your eyes. For the days will come upon
you when your enemies will throw up a barricade
against you, and surround you and hem you in on
every side, and they will level you to the ground**

> **and your children within you, and they will not leave you one stone upon another, because you did not recognize the time of your visitation.**
>
> **Luke 19:41-44 (NASB)**

Earlier he had given his men similar warnings:

> **But when you see Jerusalem surrounded by armies, then recognize that her desolation is near.**
>
> **Luke 21:20 (NASB)**

> **Woe to those who are pregnant and to those who are nursing babies in those days; for there will be great distress upon the land and wrath to this people; and they will fall by the edge of the sword, and will be led captive into all the nations; and Jerusalem will be trampled under foot by the Gentiles until the times of the Gentiles are fulfilled.**
>
> **Luke 21:23-24 (NASB)**

Let's return to the 103rd Question of Jesus of Nazareth:

> **For if these things are done when the wood is green, what will happen when it is dry?"**
>
> **Luke 23:31**

Some Biblical scholars view this question as perplexing and leave it at that, but my view is Jesus wants us to understand his questions, so let's see what this one – **"For if these things are done when the wood is green, what will happen when it is dry?"** – might mean.

Jesus liked to speak in metaphors and analogies about crops, seasons, and weather, and that is what I think he is doing here. He seems to be saying: this violence I am suffering, it is happening out of season. But imagine what violence will come upon you Jerusalemites, when the season for judgment comes. When the wood will be dry and it is the season of God's punishment upon this city! Imagine what it will be like, for if this is done to me – an innocent man sent from Heaven – imagine what punishment will fall on this city – a city guilty of killing the prophets and now the Messiah. At that time of punishment, the wood will be dry, and dry wood burns easily.

Why were people of Jerusalem destined for destruction? Because they joined in sentencing an innocent man to death, and not just an innocent man, but also God's son. The Bible tells us God's response when justice is denied. An example from Proverbs:

> **Whoever sows injustice will reap trouble; the rod of God's wrath will destroy him.**
>
> **Proverbs 22:8**

And another example from Proverbs showing the abomination Jerusalem committed by freeing Barabbas and condemning Jesus:

> **To acquit the guilty and to condemn the innocent – both are abominable to the Lord.**
>
> **Proverbs 17:15**

We may think, "When the Romans destroyed Jerusalem, it received justice for what they had done to Jesus," but here is something for us to think over: not everyone in Jerusalem wanted Jesus to be crucified, in fact, many welcomed him as the Messiah just days earlier. Also remember that Jerusalem's leaders may have manipulated the crowds to shout for Jesus to be crucified and for Barabbas to be released. Here is my point: many people in Jerusalem loved Jesus and wanted no harm to come their fellow Jew. For all we know, those who thought well of Jesus were a majority in Jerusalem, but even if they were not, even if they were only a small minority, why should they suffer along with those who crucified Jesus? My further point is this issue – was the destruction of Jerusalem collective punishment? If a just person lives among evil people, does the just person suffer along with the evil? Did the people in Jerusalem suffer collective judgment whether or not they were guilty of wanting Jesus of Nazareth crucified?

The question of collective judgment is relevant today. We can ask if millions of Germans suffered collective punishment for the sins of their Nazi government during World War II? Or consider this: Did millions of Russians suffer collective judgment in World War II for having an atheist government? Can the French, or Italian, or British people suffer collective judgment? And also consider: Can Americans come under collective judgment for the laws its government passes and enforces? Will there be collective judgment on millions of Americans for what is done in the name of personal freedom? We can come closer to understanding the answer to these questions if we study God's dealings with nations in the Bible and if we remember God's justice is perfect.

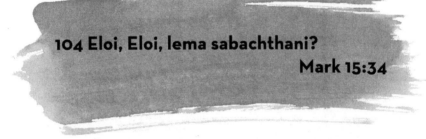

104 Eloi, Eloi, lema sabachthani?
Mark 15:34

At midday a darkness fell over the whole land, which lasted till three in the afternoon; and at three Jesus cried out with a loud voice, "Eloi, Eloi, lema sabachthani?" which means, "My God, my God, why have you forsaken Me?"

Mark 15:34

Nailed to the rigid wooden cross, his arms outstretched, spectators stare, some mock him, insulting the condemned man as he weakens and dies. The cheering crowds are gone, his friends are hiding, the governor has washed his hands of him, and it seems God has turned away from this singular Jew who said he had come to gather Israel's lost sheep. For three hours he hangs in public view, a hated man for some, but for others, a disappointment, a failed Messiah. Israel's leaders see it is a fitting end for a man who did not have their approval. For Romans, his crucifixion is a warning to anyone who thinks they can challenge the ruler of the world – Caesar.

Christians know his last words, **"My God, my God, why have You forsaken Me?"** are from the 22nd Psalm (verse 1), which continues: **"Why are you so far from saving me, so far from heeding my groans?"** (Psalm 22:1) Read the entire 22nd Psalm. It gives evidence that King David spoke prophetically of his descendent Jesus, with verse after verse describing the death of Jesus in clear prophetic detail.

Nearly every exegesis, or in plainer English, interpretation, says Jesus' words in Mark 15:34 reveal his sense of profound desolation. Possibly so, but my own interpretation differs regarding Jesus' words and the 22nd Psalm, because while this Psalm clearly describes his suffering and death, I think Jesus is telling us that his death will turn to triumph, if one remembers the later verses of the 22nd Psalm and not just the more well-known first verse. For example, note the 24th verse: **"For he has not scorned him who is downtrodden, nor shrunk in loathing from his plight, nor hidden his face from him, but he has listened to his cry for help."**

And read the conclusion of this Psalm:

> **But I shall live for his sake; my descendents will serve him.**
> **The coming generation will be told of the Lord;**
> **they will make known his righteous deeds,**
> **declaring to a people yet unborn:**
> **"The Lord has acted."**
>
> **Psalm 22:29-31**

When I read what Jesus says from the cross, **"My God, my God, why have you forsaken Me?"** I understand this is also from the 22nd Psalm, **"The Lord has acted."**

105 What is it you are debating as you walk?
Luke 24:17

"What is it you are debating as you walk?"
Luke 24:17

"What news?"
Luke 24:19

Was not the Messiah bound to suffer in this way before entering upon his glory?"
Luke 24:26

Luke's report holds a mystery and a surprise that has intrigued people ever since it was written.

The Italian painter Michelangelo Caravaggio, known for his brilliant paintings like the *Conversion of Saint Paul*, was one of those fascinated by Luke's report, and it inspired him to paint the *Supper at Emmaus*, a masterpiece capturing the moment when three men realize the identity of their dinner guest. Caravaggio's trademark technique of having subjects emerge into light from darkness is wonderfully seen in the *Supper at Emmaus*.

Luke tells of two friends of Jesus, who, shortly after his crucifixion were walking to the village of Emmaus, seven miles from Jerusalem.

As the two are walking and talking about Jesus' crucifixion, a stranger comes up alongside and asks, **"What is it you are debating as you walk?"** The two downcast men stop in their tracks and sorrowfully tell this seemingly uninformed stranger, **"Are you the only person staying in Jerusalem not to have heard the news of what has happened there in the last few days?"**

"What news?" the stranger asks.

"About Jesus of Nazareth," they replied, **"who, by deeds and words of power, proved himself a prophet in the sight of God and the whole people; and how our chief priests and rulers handed him over to be sentenced to death, and crucified him. But we had been hoping that he was to be the liberator of Israel. What is more, this is the third day since it happened, and now some women of our company have astounded us: they went early to the tomb, but failed to find his body, and returned with a story that they have seen a vision of angels who told them he was alive. Then some of our people went to the tomb and found things just as the women had said; but him they did not see."**

"How dull are you!" he answered. **"How slow to believe all the prophets said! Was not the Messiah bound to suffer in this way before entering upon his glory?"**

Luke 24:17-26

As this stranger and the two men continue walking to Emmaus, the stranger explains to them all the prophecies relating to the Messiah, beginning with Moses. Reaching Emmaus, the stranger starts to continue on, but the two men urge the stranger to stay with them in Emmaus because the evening was falling. The stranger accepts their invitation and joins them for dinner.

"And when he had sat down with them at the table, he took bread and said the blessing; he broke the bread, and offered it to them.

Then their eyes were opened, and they recognized him; but he vanished from their sight. They said to one another, 'Were not our hearts on fire as he talked with us on the road and explained the scriptures to us?'"

Luke 24:30-32

The two men rushed back to Jerusalem to tell the eleven disciples what had just happened on the road to Emmaus and how Jesus had revealed himself at the breaking of the bread.

Several questions come to mind: Why did Jesus disguise himself? Or did he? Luke wrote, "but something prevented them from recognizing him." (Luke 24:16) What was that "something"? Was it disbelief? And if it *was* their disbelief, that would be easy to understand as, only three days earlier, Jesus had been crucified, so Jesus would certainly have been the last person the two men would have expected to see.

Or did the resurrected Jesus appear physically different? Did he look like the Jesus they saw at the crucifixion – bloody and beaten? Unlikely that was the case. Or did Jesus look like someone else? In Mark's report of this event, he wrote Jesus appeared in a "different form." (Mark 16:12 NASB). What form? Did he appear as a Jew? A Roman? A Greek? An Arab? A Samaritan? Did he have a physical defect, or did he appear as a handsome young man? A friendly older man? Maybe later, when the two men described the Jesus they had met on their way to Emmaus, perhaps each described Jesus differently, as though each of the two men had seen and spoken to a different person.

Intriguing questions.

In whatever form he appeared, the two men didn't see Jesus – they saw someone else. Was it psychological blindness? There is such a phenomenon and motorcycle riders are aware of it from personal experience – people experiencing psychological blindness cannot see what they do not expect to see.

I experienced this dangerous phenomenon while riding my motorcycle. Years ago, as I rode in the left lane of a two-lane highway, the driver of the car to my right looked at me – directly at me – and then began moving into my lane, coming at me! In a split second, I thought, *"I know he saw me! ... He just looked right at me!"* But he kept coming as though I were not there – as though he hadn't seen me. I honked and accelerated my motorcycle quickly out of his way. *But because this driver did not expect to see a motorcycle – he didn't see a motorcycle*, it was as simple as that. (No, he wasn't on a cell phone or other device. This was in the pre-cell phone era.)

In the same way, since the two men walking to Emmaus didn't expect to see Jesus, they may have experienced psychological blindness, even though they were looking right at Jesus and talking with him.

There could be another reason the two men on the road to Emmaus were prevented from recognizing Jesus; maybe Jesus thought, if the two men recognized him too suddenly, they could go into shock. Perhaps Jesus didn't want to frighten them and thought he might test them instead, maybe thinking: *I will see how perceptive they are... I'll ask a few questions... talk to them like a stranger. I will see how long it takes them to realize it is their friend.*

It is also possible this episode is a simple, friendly joke between old friends. Maybe Jesus really just wanted to learn what they thought about all the events of recent days, thus, he 'appeared in a different form' to join in their conversation and hear their candid thoughts.

One type of drama is based on a mistaken identity, and here Jesus seems to be using that strategy, as though he were saying to the two men, *"All right, since you didn't recognize my destiny when I was with you – that the Messiah would suffer – I will continue to mystify you."* The two men, even after his death, still didn't grasp Jesus' mission, because we note they told the "stranger" (who was Jesus): "But we had been hoping that he was to be the liberator of Israel." I wonder what expression Jesus had on his face when he heard that? They were telling Jesus, in effect, that his death did not meet their expectations for the Messiah! Even after Jesus' preaching, teaching, and death, they still thought Jesus was supposed to have been a *political* Messiah! They wanted a Messiah to bring *political independence* from Rome – but liberating Israel from Rome would have been a trivial accomplishment, compared to the actual mission of Jesus of Nazareth – liberating all humans from death and granting his followers entrance into bliss, into Heaven.

So was the event on the road to Emmaus a lesson in perception? Jesus is unpredictable in the manner he chooses to enter lives. I attended a Bible study where a man in our group told us the Messiah had once visited him – he said he saw Jesus of Nazareth in his own home, and the man described the event with such specificity about the unusual quality of the light, and he spoke about it with such sincerity, that his testimony was believable. Is it necessary to believe someone who says they have been visited by Jesus or by angels? No, it is not, and yet every Christian is visited by the Messiah through his Word and is known by him. Jesus visits one person through the heart, another individual through their mind and reason, and yet another through their soul, and he frequently uses all three avenues of the heart, mind, and soul. The manner Jesus uses to meet someone is individual, but he will visit. **"Behold, I stand at the door and knock; if anyone hears My voice and opens the door, I will come in to him and will dine with him, and he with Me."**

Revelation 3:20 (NASB)

It is even possible Jesus may appear as an uninformed stranger who joins people as they are walking and going about their business.

106 Why are you so perturbed? Why do doubts arise in your mind?

Luke 24:38

As they were talking about all this, there he was, standing among them. Startled and terrified, they thought they were seeing a ghost. But he said, "Why are you so perturbed? Why do doubts arise in your mind? Look at my hands and feet. It is I myself. Touch me and see; no ghost has flesh and bones as you can see that I have." They were still incredulous, still astounded, for it seemed too good to be true. So he asked them, "Have you anything to eat?" They offered him a piece of fish they had cooked, which he took and ate before their eyes.

Luke 24:36-43

Have you believed because you have seen me? Blessed are those who have not seen and yet believe.

John 20:29 RSV

Again we see faith's fundamental, essential, and decisive importance. Faith walks on the border of belief, then it crosses that frontier from what we see and know, to what we trust and know. Reason unassisted by faith must remain within the boundaries of what is reasonable, but faith crosses that boundary, the boundary of mere reason, to reason with belief, where the truth is. Reason escorted by faith perceives what is beyond reason alone.

Other things exceed the boundaries of reasonable belief – things such as fantasies and fairy tales, science fiction and mythology – but they are not true – and come from the minds of women and men. Faith in the Messiah is reasonable but goes beyond reasonable belief. And yet it remains true, indeed, it is the Truth.

His frightened followers had locked themselves inside a room when Jesus appears before them and says, Shalom-Peace and asks them why they are nervous and doubt in their hearts?

They want proof he is real and not some ghost. Jesus asks if they have anything to eat. Yes, they have some cooked fish. He eats some. Ghosts don't eat.

Thomas was not there and when the others tell him, he says he cannot believe without proof. A week later in the same room, Jesus reappears:

> **Then He said to Thomas, "Reach here with your finger, and see My hands; and reach here your hand and put it into My side; and do not be unbelieving, but believing."**
> **John 20:27 (NASB)**

Thomas accepts the reality of the resurrected Jesus, who says to him:

> **"Blessed *are* they who did not see, and yet believed."**
> **John 20:29 (NASB)**

Reason unescorted by faith cannot cross the boundary of doubt. Reason accompanied by faith can perceive the Truth.

107 Why are you weeping? Who are you looking for?

John 20:15

Jesus asked her, "Why are you weeping? Who are you looking for?" Thinking it was the gardener, she said," If it is you, sir, who has removed him, tell me where you have laid him, and I will take him away." Jesus said, "Mary!" She turned and said to him, "Rabbuni!" (which is Hebrew for "Teacher").

John 20:15-16

Mary weeps and a man asks, "Woman, why are you weeping? Who are you looking for?" She thinks it's the gardener, she doesn't recognize him, but when she does, she is joyous.

Words Jesus said just days earlier become literally true:

In very truth I tell you, you will weep and mourn, but the world will be glad. But though you will be plunged in grief, your grief will be turned to joy.

John 16:20

So it is with you: for the moment you are sad; but I shall see you again, and then you will be joyful, and no one shall rob you of your joy.

John 16:22

Mary did not realize it was Jesus speaking to her *until he said her name.* In John's Gospel, Jesus said he calls his sheep by their name and they know his voice. This story shows us the Bible is interwoven with both symbolism and literalism and it is wise to ignore anyone saying it is only one or the other.

Skeptics and atheists say the Bible is a collection of ancient myths and is, therefore, irrelevant. They are wrong, of course. The Bible tells us of the past, speaks to current events and foretells future events through its inspired prophetic power. Christians know the Bible was written by humans who were moved and inspired by the Holy Spirit of God.

The Bible is God's Word. Think back to the September 11 attack against the United States because that event tells us something important about the Bible's power to inform us of the future. On the morning of that attack, enemies skyjacked four jets – two of them flew into the World Trade Center towers, killing 2,750, a third jet crashed into the Pentagon, killing 184, and a fourth jet crashed into a field in Pennsylvania because its passengers resisted the enemies' plans. That crash caused 40 more deaths. The world saw the New York towers fall and the destruction at the Pentagon, and wondered, "Why did they do this? What inspired them?" The Bible explains.

Two-thousand years ago, Jesus described the September 11 killers perfectly, in John 10:10:

> **The thief comes only to steal and kill and destroy;
> I came that they may have life, and have *it*
> abundantly.**
>

John 10:10 (NASB)

"The thief comes only to *steal and kill* and *destroy*" – those 9-11 terrorists *stole* four jets, *killed* nearly 3,000 and *destroyed* buildings.

The Bible communicates current events and points to future ones.

> God offers the opposite of those who steal, kill, and destroy, and Moses spoke of the choice between "life and prosperity" or " death and adversity." (Deuteronomy 30:15 NASB) Similarly, Jesus described his mission in this way: **I came that they may have life, and have *it* abundantly.**

Christians knew how to understand the September 11 attackers and they did not need Middle East experts or apologists to explain.

Christians knew, because they remember what Jesus said about recognizing the true nature of people:

You will know them by their fruits.
Matthew 7:16 (NASB)

Christians saw the 9-11 murderer's "fruit" – hatred and death and wars. And by their fruit we know others, despite anything they say to the world, we will know people by what they produce.

108 "Friends, have you caught anything?"
John 21:5

He called out to them, "Friends, have you caught anything?" "No." they answered. He said, "Throw the net out to the starboard, and you will make a catch." They did so, and found they could not haul the fish on board, there were so many fish in it.

John 21:5-6

The New Testament makes many references to fish.

Simon-Peter, Andrew and other disciples were fishermen.

Jesus fed 5,000 with only two fish and five loaves.
See John 6:9 / Matthew 14:17

Jesus told Peter to drop a hook into the lake and open the mouth of the first fish he caught to find a coin for the temple tax.

See Matthew 17:27

When Jesus returned to life and the disciples thought him a ghost, Jesus ate some cooked fish to prove he was not.

See Luke 24:42

After his resurrection, Jesus appears to his men one morning by the Sea of Tiberias. When they first caught sight of him, Jesus is cooking fish on a charcoal fire.

See John 21:5

One reason fish are mentioned frequently is they were caught in the Sea of Galilee and widely consumed by Jews in northern Israel. In those days, the people ate daily bread made from barley, and occasionally, chicken, but their diet was more limited than ours and consisted mainly of beans, lentils, cucumbers, leeks, onions, as well as nuts, figs, and melons. They did not have sugar, as it was then unknown, but grapes and pomegranates were eaten for sweets, and during the holidays there might be roast lamb or goat.

Jews and Romans were unaware of many of the foods we have today: tomatoes, potatoes, pasta, rice, pineapples, peanuts, and chocolate, but before pitying them for not knowing about and enjoying these foods, it may be they who pity us, because as followers of the Messiah they are now enjoying in Paradise food and drink surpassing anything even the most exclusive restaurant on earth can offer.

Now we note another failure to recognize Jesus and this time by his own disciples; and, again, Jesus' appearance and his meeting with his men centers around a meal, as it did in Emmaus.

You might have noted a couple of other things about Jesus' question to his men while they were on their boat:

"Friends, have you caught anything?"

His question closes the loop from his first meeting with Simon-Peter. According to an early chapter in Luke, when Jesus first met Simon, he asked Simon to fish; Simon is reluctant, telling Jesus he had fished all day and night without luck.

It is as though Jesus is saying to Peter, "Remember that time I asked you to fish again, but you resisted and told me you'd tried and failed?" Jesus' question may have brought back memories to Simon of when he first met Jesus.

And here again is that surprise – Jesus calls the fishermen "friends." Maybe it is possible for holy men like Augustine, Francis of Assisi, or Martin Luther to consider the Son of God a friend, but I find the Son of God calling anyone a *friend* to be astounding.

Jesus makes clear to his friends that it was his decision not theirs: "You did not choose me: I chose you." This is an encouraging thought as God's judgment is perfect.

> "You are my friends, if you do what I command you."
> John 15:14

109 Jesus said, "If I want him to remain until I come, what *is that* to you? You follow me!"

John 21:22 (NASB)

Peter, turning around, saw the disciple whom Jesus loved following *them*; the one who had also leaned back on his bosom at the supper and said, "Lord, who is the one who betrays You?"

So Peter seeing him said to Jesus, "Lord, and what about this man?" Jesus said to him, "If I want him to remain until I come, what *is that* to you? You follow Me!

John 21:20-22

Even though Peter had been given the keys of the Kingdom of Heaven, he was too curious to resist asking Jesus about the fate of the beloved disciple, who he noticed followed him and Jesus. Jesus told Peter not to worry about the fate of someone else, "What is that to you? You follow me!"

Speculating about the fate of others is not important to one's own faith and future. Jesus seems to say that we should not let curiosity regarding others concern us, but says to us, "Follow me."

110 A third time he said, "Simon son of John, do you love me?"

John 21:17

"Simon son of John, do you love me more than these others?

"Yes, Lord," he answered, "you know that I love you."

"Then feed my lambs," he said.

A second time he asked, "Simon son of John, do you love me?"

"Yes, Lord, you know I love you."

"Then tend my sheep."

A third time he said, "Simon son of John, do you love me?"

Peter was hurt that he asked a third time, "Do you love me?"

"Lord," he said, "you know everything; you know I love you."

Jesus said, "Then feed my sheep."

John 21:15-17

Why did Jesus ask Simon-Peter the same question three times? Many think Jesus asked three times to cancel out Peter's threefold rejection of Jesus on the night Jesus was arrested.

Jesus tells Peter to care for his "sheep"– those small, harmless creatures. While sheep are not highly intelligent, they have good memories and can remember a human face for years. Sheep can also pick out their own mother's wavering bleats from among the entire flock. Jesus knew of their talent for sound recognition and taught that his followers have the human equivalent of it, saying, "My own sheep listen to my voice; I know them and they follow me." (John 10:27)

Growing up in Los Angeles, the only animals I saw were dogs and cats, except for trips to the San Diego Zoo, with its incredible array of animals from every corner of the world. Jerusalem is unlike any American city and there you will occasionally see flocks of sheep.

On Saturday mornings in Jerusalem, one will find Arab shepherds buying and selling sheep just outside Jerusalem's massive walls (Friday is the Muslim Sabbath, so they conduct business as usual on Saturday, Saturday being the Jewish Sabbath, or more specifically, the Jewish Sabbath is from Friday sunset to Saturday sunset). (Note: Jerusalem has an Old City and a New City. The Old Jerusalem is walled and New Jerusalem is unwalled and extends outward from the Old Jerusalem.) Other times, as I walked near Hebrew University, I would see an Arab herdsman guide his flock, walking along side of them, as his sheep focused on one thing – eating. The sheep ambled along seemingly unaware of their direction and never raised their heads, but focused their attention downward toward any grass in their path.

As the sheep moved in a tight flock, they gently rubbed against one another, as though magnetically drawn together, bobbling along in a large cluster of white wool. Once in a while, a young lamb would skip high above the rest of the flock, as though on springs. If I watched long enough, one sheep on the flock's perimeter would be so thoroughly focused on eating that it would absentmindedly wander away, and then begin bleating, thinking itself lost, even though the flock was not far away – either it could not see its flock – or it was too petrified with fear to take the initiative to rejoin its flock. The shepherd would hear the forlorn sheep, go to it, and guide it back to his flock with his staff.

Watching these sheep, I wondered why Jesus compared his followers to them? (There are an estimated one billion sheep in the world.) Why didn't Jesus liken followers to elephants, those strong, nine-ton animals? Wouldn't elephants be more impressive symbols than sheep? Or what about comparing his followers to eagles, those regal birds with telescopic eyesight that can fly higher than any other bird. Or why not compare followers to horses? Horses – those powerful and beautiful animals that have carried men into battle and people across nations and continents.

But Jesus calls his followers sheep and liked to use that symbol in several ways.

To warn his followers against deception:

> **Beware of the false prophets, who come to you in sheep's clothing, but inwardly are ravenous wolves.**
> **Matthew 7:15 (NASB)**

To mark out his mission:

> **I was sent only to the lost sheep of the house of Israel.**
> **Matthew 15:24 (NASB)**

To describe his sympathy for wanting to learn:

> **When Jesus went ashore, He saw a large crowd, and He felt compassion for them because they were like sheep without a shepherd; and He began to teach them many things.**
> **Mark 6:34 (NASB)**

To teach followers that they should not be like sheep in all ways:

> **Behold, I send you out as sheep in the midst of wolves; so be shrewd as serpents and innocent as doves.**
> **Matthew 10:16 (NASB)**

And to cast a light on his identity:

> **I am the good shepherd; the good shepherd lays down His life for the sheep.**
> **John 10:11 (NASB)**

Jesus knew that sheep were used symbolically time and again in the Psalms and in the prophetic books.

To describe the Israelite Exodus in the Psalms:

> **But He led forth His own people like sheep**
> **And guided them in the wilderness like a flock**
> **Psalm 78:52 (NASB)**

In David's 100th Psalm:

> **Know that the Lord Himself is God;**
> **It is He who made us, and not we ourselves;**
> **_We are_ His people and the sheep of His pasture.**
> **Psalm 100:3 (NASB)**

In Ezekiel:

> **I myself shall tend my flock, and find them a place to rest, says the Lord God. I shall search for the lost, recover the straggler, bandage the injured, strengthen the sick, leave the healthy and strong to play, and give my flock their proper food.**
> **Ezekiel 34:15-16**

Isaiah 53 prophesied a man who would be accused, but not reply, suffer injury, but not retaliate. Jesus of Nazareth is the man of whom Isaiah spoke: "He was arrested and sentenced and taken away – and who gave a thought to his fate."

> **We had all strayed like sheep, each of us going his own way,**
> **but the Lord laid on him the guilt of us all.**

He was maltreated, yet he was submissive
and did not open his mouth; like a sheep led to the
slaughter,
like a ewe that is dumb before the shearers,
he did not open his mouth.

He was sentenced and taken away,
and who gave a thought to his fate –
how he was cut off from the world of the living,
stricken to death for my people's transgression?

He was assigned a grave with the wicked,
a burial-place among felons,
though he had done no violence,
had spoken no word of treachery.

Isaiah 53:6-9

The Messiah likened followers to sheep, instead of elephants, eagles, or horses. Today sheep are still raised for food, their wool, and in some religions, they are still sacrificed.

These gentle creatures symbolically represent Jesus of Nazareth's followers:

For everyone who exalts himself will be humbled;
and whoever humbles himself will be exalted.

Luke 14:11

Blessed are the gentle, for they shall inherit the
earth.

Matthew 5:5 (NASB)

Many view the Bible as just a collection of simple stories and it is true Jesus liked to teach with images and simple stories, but his stories conceal more wisdom than is detectable in a first reading and 20

245

centuries later we are still exploring and wondering at the depth and brilliance of Jesus' questions.

The Messiah's mission was to Jews first, but after his resurrection his mission expanded to all people, and the core teaching of his mission can be found in these seven words that King David had earlier revealed:

> **Trust in the Lord and do good.**
>
> Psalm 37:3

Remember the lawyer who asked Jesus, "Teacher, what must I do to inherent eternal life?" Jesus said, "What is written in the Law? What is your reading of it?" (Luke 10:25-26) In effect saying to the lawyer: if you understand the law, you already know the answer.

The lawyer said:

> **Love the Lord your God with all your heart, and all your soul, and all your strength, and with all your mind; and your neighbor as yourself.**
>
> **That is the right answer, said Jesus; do that and you will have life.**
>
> **Luke 10:27-28**

Those living on Earth are born to understand that question and to give the right answer.

Here this book ends.

About the Author

Ben-Joseph has written for White House cabinet members, members of Congress, political party leaders, government public affairs offices, and for scientific organizations.

He studied Judaism and Christianity for many years on both the East and West coasts of the United States. At the Hebrew University of Jerusalem, Israel, the California State University at Long Beach, and the Georgetown University in Washington, D.C.

A native of California, Ben-Joseph currently lives in the Mid-Atlantic region of the U.S.

More of his writing can be found at jonahbenjoseph.com

Made in the USA
Middletown, DE
01 November 2022

13902925R00158